John Audubon
and the World of Birds for Kids

MICHAEL ELSOHN ROSS

CHICAGO REVIEW PRESS

Published by Chicago Review Press, Incorporated
814 North Franklin Street
Chicago, Illinois 60610
ISBN 978-1-64160-618-9

Library of Congress Control Number: 2022938190

Cover and interior design: Sarah Olson
Cover images: (*front cover*) Portrait of Audubon by John Syme, 1826, WikiCommons; Flatboat, Historic New Orleans Collection, WikiCommons; Whip-poor-will, American white pelican, raven, ruffed grouse, belted kingfisher, and Carolina parakeet, *Birds of America*; (*back cover*) Mallard ducks, roseate spoonbill, black-billed cuckoos, and white ibis, *Birds of America*

Unless otherwise noted, interior illustrations are from John James Audubon's *Birds of America*. Thanks to art curator Alexandra Copeland, who generously gave me her time in allowing me to look through the pages of the copy of the *Birds of America* elephant folio in the collection of the New Bedford Free Public Library, New Bedford, Massachusetts.

Printed in the United States of America
5 4 3 2 1

To my two granddaughters,
who have loved the birds from
the earliest age, and my wife, Lisa,
my daily birding companion.

CONTENTS

· · · · · · · · · · · ·

TIME LINE

• • • • • • • • • • • •

1785 April 26, Jean Rabin (John James Audubon) born in Les Cayes, St. Dominique (now Haiti)

1788 Young Jean Rabin arrives at Nantes, France

1789 May 5, French Revolution begins

1791 August 22, Haitian Revolution begins

1799 November, French Revolution ends

1803 August, Audubon arrives in New York and changes his name from Jean Jacques to John James

1804 Winter, John James Audubon and Lucy Bakewell fall in love

1805 March, Audubon departs for France

1806 May 28, Audubon returns from France with Ferdinand Rozier

June 4, Reunites with Lucy Bakewell

1807 August 31, Audubon and Rozier leave for Louisville, Kentucky, to open store

1808 April 5, Audubon and Bakewell marry

1809 June 12, Victor Gifford Audubon is born

1812 June 18, War of 1812 begins

November 30, John Woodhouse Audubon born

1818 February 18, John James's father dies in France

1819 Nationwide financial panic; John James goes bankrupt

Autumn, daughter Rose Audubon is born

1820 Winter, baby Rose dies

Autumn, John James departs for the South with student Robert Mason to illustrate birds

1821 John James Audubon teaches art and paints portraits

Lucy and boys join John James in New Orleans

1826 Audubon departs New Orleans for England

July 21, arrives in Liverpool

Autumn, successful exhibition of paintings in Liverpool

1827 April 5, leaves for London

Printers Robert Havell and Sons agree to print book

1828 Audubon travels around England seeking subscribers

1829 Mid-May to mid-September, paints birds in Northeast

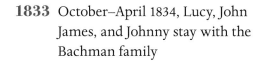

November 17, Reunites with Lucy at Beechwood Estate, Louisiana

1830 October, Audubon begins working in Edinburgh with Lucy and William MacGillivray on Volume 1 of *Ornithological Biography*

Elected a Fellow of the Royal Society of London

1831 October, Audubon leaves for expedition to Florida

Befriends John Bachman

1832 April, Audubon and assistants return to Florida and visit the Keys

June, John James, Lucy, and sons travel to Maine and New Brunswick

August, John James, Lucy, and son Johnny settle in Boston for winter

1833 June 6, Audubon, John Woodhouse, and young assistants depart Eastport, Maine, for Labrador trip

August 31, Return to Eastport

1833 October–April 1834, Lucy, John James, and Johnny stay with the Bachman family

1835 June, John James, and Lucy go to Edinburgh to work on *Ornithological Biography*

1836 August 2, Audubon returns to New York for skins from Nuttall/Townsend western expedition

1837 February 17, Audubon, Bachman, and Edward Harris leave on expedition to Gulf Coast of Texas

1838 Mid-April, Audubon completes his last hundred drawings for *Birds of America*

1839 *Birds of America* completed

Spring, Audubon buys acreage in upper Manhattan Island

1842 Audubon family moves to house built on Minnie's Land, his new estate

1844 Octavo edition of *Birds of America* (in seven volumes) published

1847 Audubon has light stroke; onset of dementia

1851 January 27, Audubon dies at home on Minnie's Land

INTRODUCTION

· · · · · · · · · · ·

In the riverfront town of Henderson, Kentucky, John James Audubon and his wife, Lucy, were the talk of the town. In the morning you could see them riding horses together. In summer you could watch them swim the half-mile (0.8 km) across the Ohio River to the Indiana shore. Audubon, being a fine marksman, routinely won first place at shooting competitions. He raced others on horseback down the streets, often leaving his opponents in the dust.

Audubon was an excellent swordsman as well. His bravery was legendary. He assisted the sheriff in arresting a "river pirate." When the man attacked him with a "long, murderous-looking knife," Audubon grabbed an oar and wacked him so hard that he cracked the man's skull. The incapacitated criminal was then hauled off to jail. Audubon was regarded as a "man of scrupulous honesty" and so generous that other men would sometimes take advantage of his generosity.

During his years exploring for birds and shooting them for drawing, he sometimes found his life in danger. A great horned owl he drew on the last day of September 1814 he had shot near a river. He nearly lost his life when it fell onto a sandbar, and he leapt onto the sand to retrieve its body. Audubon wrote, "I suddenly found myself sunk in quicksand up to my arm-pits, and in this condition must have remained to perish, had not my boatmen come up and extricated me, by forming a bridge of their oars and some driftwood, during which operation I had to remain perfectly quiet, as any struggle would soon have caused me to sink overhead."

Had that occurred, John James Audubon never would have accomplished his great work of describing and picturing the birds of America.

1

A REVOLUTIONARY CHILDHOOD

....

John James Audubon was the son of a pirate. His father, Jean Audubon, was from a long line of seafaring men. He was the captain of a merchant ship and a privateer (a pirate licensed by his country to attack and plunder ships from enemy nations). He spent much time on the Caribbean French colony of St. Dominique where he had many friends.

Black-crowned night herons.

Jean Audubon had married Anne Moynet, a well-to-do French childless widow. Being 14 years older than him, she was not likely to bear children. He had daughters with Sanitte, a free Black woman he lived with in St. Dominique but was not married to. She was the eldest daughter of a French plantation owner and his Black mistress. Having children with someone from another race was common in the colonies but considered a disgrace in France.

As a privateer, licensed by the French king, Captain Audubon was able to keep part of the plunder and a portion of the money from the sale of captured Spanish and English ships. He transported goods such as wine and passengers from France. He also traded and transported slaves. With his loot, Audubon bought a sugar plantation in Perche near Les Cayes, St. Dominique. It had a sugar refinery and storehouse, where slaves did all the hard work.

One of his passengers was a very beautiful 25-year-old French chambermaid by the name of Jeanne Rabin. In 1784 she became pregnant with their son, who was born on April 26, 1785. By November she died from tropical fevers and infections, leaving her baby son Jean Rabin motherless. Since he was born out of wedlock (by parents not married to each other), he bore his mother's surname. He was neither entitled to bear his father's name nor to inherit from him. Baby Jean was cared for by Sanitte and his older half-sisters. He seldom saw his father, who was often at sea.

Revolt

During young Jean's first years he listened to the sounds of squealing parrots, squawking night herons, and gurgling palm chats. Later in life he would remember the call of a black bird, the smooth billed ani, that sounded like it was saying *un petit bout de petun* (a little roll of tobacco).

The people young Jean grew up with spoke French, Yoruba, and a variety of other African languages. He was accustomed to the gentle voice of Sanitte, his Afro-French caretaker, and the harsh commands of overseers on his father's sugar plantation. The cries of slaves beaten by overseers was a sound he would try to forget. Jean Rabin, later

Smooth billed ani.
Charles J. Sharp,
WikiCommons

to be known as John James Audubon, lived on the plantation for the first three years of his life. For much of this time his father was away on his ship or staying with his wife Anne, who was living in Nantes, France. In April 1787, Sanitte gave birth to Jean's third half-sister, Rose.

Jean first developed a love of plants and animals on this tropical island with its intense heat and drenching rains. It would have been a paradise if not for the cruel colonial rule of Spain and France. For 100 years the French had been bringing slaves from West Africa, and by the time of Jean's birth, St. Dominique had the largest number of slaves in the Caribbean. There were more than ten times the number of slaves as French colonists. It was also the wealthiest colony, due the hard work of slaves who were treated cruelly. Plantation owners became rich from slave labor. Among these owners was Jean's father who also bought and sold slaves.

The time was ripe for a revolt. By 1788, sensing that a slave rebellion might soon occur, Captain Audubon decided to sell his plantation. He was determined to keep his only son, Jean Rabin, safe from danger. In July 1788 Jean Rabin boarded a ship bound for France, captained by an old friend of his father. Leaving his caretaker Sanitte and three half-sisters may have been heart-wrenching for such a small child. The long voyage across the Atlantic was traumatic. Later in life he would have horrible fears of dying while on transoceanic voyages.

He arrived in Nantes only weeks after the French Revolution began with the storming of the

Listen to Birds

Birdsong is an element of our soundscapes that is like a soundtrack for our memories. We hear birds without listening carefully to the details of their voices.

Now it's your chance to pay attention to them and test your listening skills. Visit a relatively quiet outdoor space in the morning. Find a comfortable place to sit and listen. You will hear bird calls, single or several notes, such as the *caw caw* of a crow or the single *tup* or *tut, tut, tut* of an American robin. Birdsongs are a repeated series of notes, a musical tune, such as an American robin's *cheer up, cheer up, cheerily* song or a red-winged blackbird's liquid, gurgling, *konk-la-reee*.

When you hear birds, try to determine where they are singing, and if they are not visible, listen to discover what direction their song is coming from. Try to tell if more than one bird is singing. How many individual birds do you think you hear? How many different birdsongs do you think you hear?

dreaded prison, the Bastille, and the release of its prisoners. Though less than 250 miles (402 km) away, Nantes was still peaceful. Anne Moynet, his father's wife, warmly welcomed young Jean. At 54 years of age, she relished the role of mothering the handsome and bright young boy.

In 1789 Captain Audubon sent for his youngest daughter, Rose, who was fair skinned enough to pass as white. For entry into France, she was given the name Rose Rabin, daughter of the dead Frenchwoman, Jeanne Rabin. She and Jean's older half-sisters, with their mother's darker skin, obviously had African blood, and it would be improper in French society for Captain Audubon to claim them as his own.

Haitian Revolution. *WikiCommons*

Among the slaves in St. Dominique were courageous leaders who secretly planned a revolution. In 1789, Jean Audubon sold sugar from his warehouse and bought a large farm near Philadelphia, Pennsylvania, in case a rebellion occurred. On August 22, 1791, the slaves overthrew their masters and liberated themselves, killing many of the plantation masters and their families. In Les Cayes 50 colonists lost their lives. One of them was Audubon's eldest daughter, 16-year-old Marie-Madeleine, but Sanitte and her other child escaped without harm. The revolutionaries took over St. Dominique. They would battle the French for another 12 years before they could finally establish their own country called Haiti, a name based on the original Taino-Arawak name Ay-ti, meaning "land of mountains."

In March 1794, the French Revolution's reign of terror finally reached Nantes, when 160 Catholic priests were drowned in the river Loire. Within the next year as many as 4,000 more "enemies of the revolution" were killed by drowning. Living less than a 10-minute walk from the river, the children may have witnessed these horrific scenes.

With violence sweeping the nation, Captain Audubon was worried about the fate of his children if he and Anne lost their lives, so they formally adopted the children. Since the Catholic church had been outlawed by the revolutionaries, so were Christian first names. Jean was now called Jean Jacques Fougere (fern) Audubon and Rose was now Rose Muguet (lily of the valley) Audubon.

Their country home La Gerbetière, in Couëron, eight miles (1.6 km) down the Loire River from Nantes, was situated on the edge of the

Bird-Watching Journal

Audubon gave advice about keeping notes in a journal: "Leave nothing to memory, but note down all your observations with ink, not with a black-lead pencil; and keep in mind the more particulars you write at the time, the more you will afterword recollect." Over his many years of keeping journals Audubon wrote hundreds of pages of observations.

The Bird-Watching Journal you start in this activity will be essential for other activities in this book. Every time you make bird observations, you will record them in this journal.

YOU WILL NEED:

↘ A notebook, preferably unlined paper

↘ Pen or pencil

Your Bird-Watching Journal is a place to keep your thoughts and questions about birds. For example, "A robin was poking in the grass. What was it searching for?" Write this question down. Then, over time, you may find the answer to that question, or have additional questions, such as, "Is it looking for worms?" Write about *everything* you observe or question.

Always be sure to write the date, time, and location of each entry. For example, "May 25, 9 AM, in front of my house." This will help you keep track of which birds are present in your local environment, and when.

Keep your Bird-Watching Journal handy—throughout this book, you will be asked to record your observations of local species.

WHAT IS A BIRD?

What makes a bird a bird? Instead of teeth, birds have bills, also known as beaks. Instead of arms, they have wings, though not all of them use the wings for flight. The wings of a penguin are like paddles that aid it in swimming, and the wings of an ostrich help it balance as it runs. Instead of being born a live baby, a bird hatches out of an egg. Instead having hair, birds have feathers, also known as plumage. Birds also have scaly skin like reptiles on their legs, feet, and around their eyes.

Birds may be as small as a bumble bee or taller than a human. They may be brown, blue, red, or a combination of many colors. Their bills may be long as a flute or as short as a pencil tip. Their legs may be the size of those of a mouse or as tall as those of teenager. Think about the birds you have seen where you live. What size and color are they? How long are their legs and bills?

Blue-headed pigeon.

The Audubon's house in Couëron on the banks of the Loire River, currently a cultural center.
WikiCommons

village with a view of the river. To young Jean it was a magical place. Jean, especially, was indulged by Madam Audubon. She was old enough to be their grandmother and like a grandmother spoiled her children. She let Jean buy sweets in the village whenever he wished. She allowed him to freely roam the neighboring fields and marshes. Birds were everywhere and fascinated Jean.

"I felt an intimacy with them . . . bordering on a frenzy [that] must accompany my steps through life," he wrote later in life.

A Young Artist

At the age of seven young Jean started drawing birds and eventually created over 200 sketches.

His father also had a love of birds, and Jean remembered, "He would point out the elegant movement of birds, and the beauty and softness of their plumage. He called my attention to their show of pleasure or sense of danger, their perfect forms and splendid attire."

Each day, Jean took off for school carrying the basket of food his stepmother had packed for his school lunch. When his father was away at sea, Jean would explore in the fields and marshes all day instead of going to school and return with the basket containing bird nests, special stones, bits of moss, and other items of interest. His bedroom became a small nature museum with all these "curiosities" on display. When his father returned from his trips he was impressed by his son's vast collection, but unhappy with his lack of progress in math and other subjects.

Captain Audubon wished for Jean Jacques to be prepared for the future and forced him to attend school, which bored him. In those days, students had to learn by repeating the teacher's every word and memorizing what they were told or read. Jean was an active learner who learned best by doing, not just listening. Later in life this would be a trait that would bring him success as an explorer.

Hoping his son would become a naval officer, Captain Audubon decided an education in mathematics, geography, drawing, music, and fencing was needed. For music he hired a talented teacher who taught Jean to skillfully play the violin, flageolet (a type of flute), and guitar. For art instruction he employed a student of the famous painter Jacques Louis David, who taught Jean to trace

Draw a Bird

Drawing helps you see better, and as you see better your drawings will improve.

YOU WILL NEED:

↓ Bird-Watching Journal

↓ Pencil

↓ Colored pencils (optional)

Picture a bird in your mind and then draw it, making it large enough to cover most of a blank journal page.

Next, draw one of the birds you are familiar with. Pay attention to its shape, size, and color. Think about the relative size of the bill, legs, wings, and other body parts. Do you have questions about the features of the bird you have chosen to draw? Would it be easier if you had the bird in view?

Using a Bird Field Guide

There were few books with illustrations in Audubon's day, and they were too expensive and too big to carry around. All he had was a list of birds from Alexander Wilson and descriptions he could read at a special library that carried Wilson's American Ornithology.

A field guide to birds of North America, or the specific region where you live, will provide you with pictures to compare what you observed. The Sibley, Kaufman, Peterson, and National Geographic field guides contain illustrations emphasizing key visual characteristics, known as field marks.

YOU WILL NEED:

↘ Bird field guide
↘ Bird-Watching Journal
↘ Pen or pencil

Check out different field guides from your library to see which one you like best before buying your own copy. Some field guides to birds use photographs. These are not as useful for seeing important details that can be shown more clearly in an illustration.

Look carefully through each guide. A field guide to birds will have information on identification, songs and calls, and maps showing where the birds can be found during nesting, wintering, and migration periods. Birds are arranged in groups such as gulls, ducks, hawks, thrushes, warblers, and sparrows. There are pointers on telling the difference between similar species, such as a Western and Eastern Bluebird. Familiarize yourself with these bird groups by browsing through the book.

Carry your field guide with you in a pack when you are outdoors looking for birds, so you will be prepared when you come across one that is new to you. Record your discoveries in your Bird-Watching Journal.

natural objects and create dramatic compositions. Jean also learned to dance. Though his father's intent was for these skills to serve him as a naval officer, they later became essential in supporting Jean's passion for picturing birds. It would be two centuries before there were guides available to assist birdwatchers in identifying bird species in the field.

At age 12, Jean Jacques was sent off to military school and assigned as a cabin boy on a navy ship. The constant rocking of the ship made him seasick. He lacked talent or interest in math and navigation. Though it was no surprise, after four years of schooling he failed the officer's qualification test.

After Napoleon Bonaparte became emperor of France and set his sights on conquering Europe, Captain Audubon feared that his son would be drafted to serve on the frontlines and perish in battle. He sent Jean Jacques across the sea, with a false passport, for a new life in America to Mill Grove, his farm in Pennsylvania.

The estate was managed by a Quaker tenant named William Thomas. Before young Audubon's departure, Frenchman Francis Dacosta had been sent by Captain Audubon to examine a deposit of lead ore discovered at Mill Grove and, if worthwhile, develop a mine. He was also assigned the duty of looking after Jean.

2

NEW WORLD, NEW LIFE

············

Following the six-week-long crossing of the Atlantic, Jean Jacques reached the wharves of New York City in August 1803. He was four months past his 18th birthday and both charming and handsome. For his new life he had changed his name to the English equivalent, John James.

Wild turkey.

Just off board, on his way to a bank to collect funds, he became almost too weak to walk. He had possibly contracted yellow fever, a virus transmitted by mosquitoes. In 1798 almost one out of twenty New York City residents had died from it. Now in the summer of 1803 it was plaguing the city once more. John James's condition was noted by the ship's captain, who had him transported to a boardinghouse outside Philadelphia where two Quaker women cared for him.

As Audubon healed, he learned some English, but it was the Quaker version that used words like *thou* and *thee*. By the time he healed fully and reached his father's estate, Mill Grove, he knew only a little English. He moved into the home of the Quaker tenant and his family. With an allow-ance of $1,600 a year (roughly $40,000 in 2022), John James led a comfortable life.

"Hunting, fishing, drawing, and music occupied my every moment. Cares I knew not, and cared naught about them," he later wrote.

An English family had just moved into a larger estate, called Fatland Ford, up the hill from Mill Grove. In November Audubon went there to find out where to buy a horse. William Bakewell, the owner of the plantation, greeted him and his friend General Andrew Porter, visiting from nearby Norristown, and was able to help.

In January, Audubon returned to Fatland Ford. William Bakewell was outdoors doing chores, so he was greeted by Bakewell's elder daughter Lucy, who was sitting in the parlor. "And there I sat, my

(left) **The New York waterfront teemed with activity.** *WikiCommons*

(right) **Mill Grove.** *Montgomery County Planning Commission, WikiCommons*

gaze riveted, as it were, on the young girl before me, who, half working, half talking, essayed to make the time pleasant to me."

Lucy was two days shy of 17. The attraction was mutual. He was handsome and enthusiastic; she was striking in appearance with her smoke-gray eyes and tall willowy figure.

During the following months, John James was a frequent visitor at Fatland Ford, and even helped with plowing and spring planting. Most importantly, his friendship with Lucy blossomed. They were a good match. Together they played music and discussed books. She offered to help improve his English, and he helped with her French. They went on long walks and horseback rides.

As the weather warmed, he discovered she was also a strong swimmer. She was kind, intelligent, meticulous, and loyal. At 18 he had met his "best friend," and she had met a man who appreciated her mind and sense of adventure.

The Young Ornithologist

Audubon remained passionate about investigating the natural world, particularly observing, collecting, mounting, and drawing birds. Just as few people today have qualms about catching fish for eating, few in Audubon's time were concerned about hunting birds for food or study. People not only ate larger birds like turkeys or ducks, but also dined on songbirds such as robins. (Today hunting songbirds is prohibited by law.) Ornithologists did not have binoculars to watch birds or cameras to photograph them, so they needed birds in hand for

WHAT'S IN A NAME?

For millennia people around the planet have given names to plants and animals in their local area. Indigenous people have had a long time to "know" their local plants and animals. In the 1940s the Eastern Band of Cherokee Indians of Qualla Reservation, North Carolina, were the only indigenous people in the Southeastern United States who still occupied their ancestral home. Anthropologist John Witthoft interviewed elders known for their bird knowledge. He showed them pictures of local birds, and they told him the Cherokee names for 100 of the species. The red-tailed hawk is called *uwes'la'oski*, or "lovesick," because its call sounds heartbroken.

Another bird was given a name that sounded like its song, *tsïkïlïlï*. A word that imitates a sound is known as an onomatopoeia. A bird that Audubon called a black capt titmouse is now known as a black-capped chickadee. Chickadee is an onomatopoeia thought to come from the Cherokee name *tsïkïlïlï*. If Audubon collected a bird new to science, he would give it a scientific and common name and be considered its discoverer. Sadly, like many naturalists, he would not have thought to ask indigenous people their names for birds or what they knew of their habits.

Chickadees.

Hunting with Your Eyes

Learn how to use binoculars to bird watch.

YOU WILL NEED:

⤵ Binoculars, preferably 8 × 40

⤵ Soft cotton cloth

⤵ Bird-Watching Journal

⤵ Pen or pencil

Before using the binoculars, clean the glass eyepieces by wiping them with a soft cotton cloth, such as a cotton handkerchief.

If you wear eyeglasses, you will need to adjust your binoculars so you can keep the glasses on. Most binoculars have a rubber eyecup around each eyepiece. If your binoculars have them, simply fold them back. Other binoculars have eyepieces that can be pulled out or pushed in. Keep them in the pushed-in position.

Adjust the distance between the two barrels of the binoculars so that they are the right width for your eyes. Too far apart or too close together will cause you to see black edges in your field of view. If you have the spacing right, your view will be a perfect circle.

Examine the two eyepieces. You should notice that at the base of the right one is a ring with numbers or markings. Make sure it is adjusted at zero. You do this by making sure the long mark is matched up with the dot below the ring. Look just with your left eyepiece at a stationary object and then focus with the central focus ring or lever. Then, using your right eye, look through the right eyepiece. If it is not in focus, move the ring until you get in focus. Look at the ring to see where the marks or numbers are and always keep that setting. Record the setting in your Bird-Watching Journal.

To quickly get focused, look at something nearby with letters or numbers, such as a sign or car license plate that you can't read with your naked eyes. Next, while keeping your eyes locked on it, bring the binoculars up to your eyes at the angle of your line of vision and focus. Repeat over and over until you get "on it" faster and faster.

Now try to get a bird in your sights. If there is a bird on the ground, fix your eyes on it and without moving your head bring the binoculars up to your eyes. You should have the bird in view. If not, lower the binoculars, and bring them up again at the same angle as your sight line. If the bird moves out of your view, lower the binoculars and find it with your naked eyes before getting "on it" with the binoculars again.

What were you able to see with the binoculars that you were not able to see with your naked eye? Record your observations in your Bird-Watching Journal.

close observation. Many ornithologists hired hunters to get specimens, but because Audubon was an excellent marksman, he did his own shooting.

On a cool morning during Audubon's first April at Mill Grove, he entered a small cave he had noticed before above Perkiomen Creek. There he had previously found a nest made of mud and grass. Two eastern phoebes—he called them flycatcher pewees—flew out. Audubon returned day after day to observe and sketch the birds, keeping notes on when the refurbishing of the old nest was completed. He also noted the appearance of the eggs, the birds' hatching, and the fledging of the young.

All of this close observation led to a new way of depicting birds. Audubon created dozens of outlines of the phoebes, and he imagined himself taking the first step to a much higher level of drawing. He wished to develop a way to pose birds he had killed for models.

Meanwhile he wondered about the newly fledged young phoebes. He knew the birds left in winter and wondered if the young would return to the same area. Another idea struck: "I fixed, a light silver thread on the leg of each, loose enough not to hurt the part, but so fastened that no exertions of theirs could remove it." He hoped the birds marked with the silver thread would show up the next year. Two springs later he found phoebes bearing the silver thread nesting farther up the creek. Thus he discovered that at least some of the offspring of this migratory songbird returned to the region of their birth to nest.

Eastern phoebes.

How to Identify a Bird

This is how Audubon described the iridescent colors of the common grackle: "The genial rays of the sun shine on their silky plumage, and offer to the ploughman's eye such rich and varying tints, that no painter, however gifted, could ever imitate them. The coppery bronze, which in one light shews its rich gloss, is, by the least motion of the bird, changed in a moment to brilliant and deep azure, and again, in the next light, becomes refulgent sapphire or emerald-green."

Like Audubon you can use words to paint a picture of a bird. When you view a bird you have not seen before and don't know the name of, you can jot down characteristics, such as color, size, shape, and behavior. This will help you to know the bird better and really see it well enough to recognize a picture of it in your field guide.

YOU WILL NEED:

↘ Bird-Watching Journal

↘ Pen or pencil

↘ Bird field guide for your region

↘ Binoculars (optional)

Look! What's that bird? How do you learn the name of a bird when there is not an expert bird-watcher like Audubon to tell you? Even experts have to use methods and tools to help them figure out which bird they are seeing.

To start, observe a bird's distinguishing features and record your findings in your Bird-Watching Journal. Such as:

Size, Shape, and Posture: Size is relative. Is the bird bigger than a small sparrow? Is it bigger than a jay? Is it bigger than a pigeon? Is it smaller than a goose?

Color Pattern: Use the bird body diagram (page 33) to describe what colors you see and where they are. For example, *It has a yellow crown and white wing bars.*

Behavior: What is the bird doing? How does it move? Is it by itself or in a small group of birds (a flock) that look alike? For example, *It hops along the ground with others that look the same, and they all fly a short distance ahead if I get too close.*

Sounds: Is it making any sounds? Are they soft or loud? Are they harsh or musical? For example, *It toots like a horn.*

Habitat: Where do you see it? Is it in the forest, in a field, on the shore, or in the water? For example, *It sits in the water and stands on the shore.*

Now look through your field guide to see if you can find the bird you have described. If you have neighbors or friends who know birds, show them your notes, and maybe they can help identify it. The more birds you observe, the more you can compare them and the better you will become at discovering their identity.

Bird Banding or Ringing

Lucy Bakewell joined Audubon on visits to the cave. Mr. Bakewell warned her about spending too much time with him, but their hours together outdoors drew them closer. It was at the cave that Lucy first expressed her feelings for him.

Lucy's father was not happy with her relationship with Audubon. He did not share the rest of his family's affection for Audubon, so he sent Lucy to New York to stay with her aunt for a month. During her absence Audubon continued to visit Fatland Ford. He hunted with Tom Bakewell and played music. During that time, Lucy's mother shared with him a letter from her daughter in New York.

Meanwhile, tensions had grown between Francis Dacosta and Audubon. Neither liked or respected the other. Dacosta said that Audubon's affection for Bakewell was, "rash and inconsiderate." Dacosta stopped the payment of Audubon's monthly allowance. Not only that, but Dacosta told Bakewell's father that Captain Audubon did not approve of his son marrying. The captain had gotten the impression from Dacosta that Mr. Bakewell was after money under the mistaken belief that John James was heir to a large fortune.

Meanwhile John James passionately pursued his dream of creating more natural pictures of birds. "Nothing, after all, could ever answer my enthusiastic desire to represent Nature, alive and moving, except to copy her in her own way." One day he finally found a solution for arranging dead birds in more lifelike poses. He bought wire, found a pine board, and then went down to the creek with his gun knowing he would find a kingfisher there. After shooting it, he returned home and set about arranging it as if in flight, using the wire to attach it to the board. With wings outstretched, as if it were about to dive after a fish, it felt like a live model. Now he was able to create more lifelike bird portraits!

Belted kingfishers.

Observe Bird Banding

To keep tabs on individual birds, ornithologists attach small, numbered bands to the legs or wings of wild birds that are captured in live traps or nets specially designed to catch birds without killing or harming them. Once in the hand, each bird is measured, its species identified, its sex and relative age determined. All the data is recorded and later sent on to the US Banding Laboratory for birds banded in the United States and Canada.

Bird bands are sometimes recovered in places far away from the banding station. An adult male Baltimore Oriole banded in Edmonton, Alberta, Canada, was recovered after crashing into a window and dying in Sevillano, Colombia, over 3,635 miles (5,850 km) away! Since the 1990s electronic chips have been used to track individual birds, providing more precise information to ornithologists, such as the number of days taken to travel to wintering sites.

There are many banding/ringing stations around the world, and some allow visitors to watch bird banders at work. Check out these websites for information about banding stations in the United States:

www.westernbirdbanding.org/banding.html
www.easternbirdbanding.org/why-band-birds/

and the United Kingdom and Ireland:

www.bto.org/our-science/projects/ringing/ringing-groups

If you have a chance to visit a banding station, write about the experience in your Bird-Watching Journal and record any questions you might have.

A researcher attaches a metal band to the leg of a common yellowthroat. *Lorie Shaull, WikiCommons*

Off to France

Before summer's end in 1804, Audubon asked William Bakewell for Lucy's hand in marriage. William's feelings had softened for Audubon, and he now thought he would make a suitable husband. In answer he said they must wait until they had approval from John James's father.

After Lucy's return from New York, they continued their relationship, spending long hours outdoors and playing music in the evening. She and John James decided that he needed to visit his father in France to convince him to bless the marriage.

As summer came to an end, Mrs. Bakewell became ill. For weeks, her husband, Lucy, and the doctor did all they could to keep her alive. Despite their efforts, she died on the last day of September. Afterward, Lucy and John James saw little of each other. The family was deep in mourning, and John James was preparing for his trip to France.

One day in early December he went off duck hunting with one of Lucy's brothers and friends. On the way home at dusk, when he was in the lead, he fell through a hole in thin ice.

"Down it I went, and soon felt the power of a most chilling bath," he recalled. "My senses must, for aught I know, have left me for a while; be this as it may, I must have glided with the stream some thirty or forty yards, when, as God would have it, up I popped at another air-hole, and here I did, in some way or another, manage to crawl out."

Soon after, John James came down with a terrible fever and was nursed back to health at Fatland

Ford by Lucy, who was constantly at his side. As he lay in bed recovering, Lucy read to him, and as he gained strength, he had time to sketch.

In March John James boarded a ship for France to visit his family, plead for his father's permission to marry Lucy, and warn him of Dacosta's deceit.

His father cautioned him to stay away from Nantes and avoid being seen by neighbors, as he was still in danger of being drafted into the military. It felt confining to have to keep out of sight, but he was still able to secretly roam the marshes and forests that bordered his home.

Dr. Charles d'Orbigny, the family physician and a passionate naturalist as well, often joined

---

JOURNALING

• • • • • •

Observe and Draw

Birds differ in the color of their plumage, bills, and legs. Some, like sparrows, are mostly brown, while others, such as jays, are mostly blue. They differ in the size of their bodies and the length of their bills, wings, tails, and legs. Some like Canada Geese are as tall as a young child, while others such as chickadees could fit in an adult's hand.

Examine a familiar bird closely. What colors do you notice in the plumage, bill, and legs? Does the bird have any special feature to its form such a crest, a point of feathers, on the head? Take notes in your Bird-Watching Journal. Now sketch!

Great spotted woodpecker, one of the birds Audubon painted while in France.

him to watch and collect birds. He also introduced John James to scientific methods, such as carefully weighing and measuring specimens. Together they dissected dead birds to examine their anatomy and stomach contents. As promised to Lucy, John James created watercolor paintings of the local birds, such as the nightingale and a great spotted woodpecker.

Both Lucy's father and his father were concerned about his ability to earn a sufficient income to support a wife and family. Both were impressed by his skill and passion as an artist and student of birdlife, but neither of them understood that he had a special calling in life. John James Audubon was destined to be a great artist and ornithologist. Lucy saw his talent and admired it. Fortunately, she was a woman who relished adventure and could endure hardship.

Despite Lucy's lessons, John James struggled with English. An excerpt from a letter to Lucy's father shows his comical mistakes: "I am here in the Snears of the eagle he will pluck Me a little and then I shall Sail on a Sheep have good wind all the way." In other words, he is saying he is in danger of being snared by the French government to serve in the military, but he will evade them to sail on a ship back to America. Though English was his second language, one day he would be regarded as an exceptional writer in that language.

While John James quietly explored the bird life, Captain Audubon worked out a plan with his friend Claude Rozier to get their sons out of France and into a business partnership in America. Ferdinand Rozier, eight years older than John

James, had more business smarts than young Audubon. The fathers drew up a contract for the sons to sign, agreeing they would be in partnership for nine years, co-own one half of Mill Grove, oversee Dacosta's work on the lead mine, and soon be able to open a store together near the frontier in Louisville, Kentucky.

On April 12, 1806, Ferdinand and John James used false passports to board an American ship bound for New York. During the journey English privateers attacked their ship. Fortunately, John James cleverly hid their money wrapped in old clothes under a reel of cable. He couldn't wait to get to Mill Grove and be with Lucy.

3

ABUNDANCE

....

The residents of Louisville welcomed Rozier and Audubon's new store. By spring, the now successful Audubon returned to Fatland Ford to marry Lucy Bakewell on April 5, 1808. He was almost 23, and she was now 21. Within three days after the wedding, they were traveling the rugged road to Pittsburgh, up and over mountains, through dust and mud. At night they stayed at inns that were crowded and dirty, with barely edible meals. Spit from numerous tobacco chewers often landed on other lodgers.

Bald eagle with catfish. Audubon called it the white-headed eagle.

John James could sleep outdoors and fast when no food was available. Lucy, not used to these hardships, showed a toughness no one knew she possessed. In her letters to family, there was no mention of these foul conditions. On a steep passage the coach she was riding in turned over and was dragged a short distance before the horse could be stopped. Lucy was bruised and battered but did not break any bones. For the remainder of the journey, every jarring movement, as the coach rolled over rocks, caused her pain.

With relief, the couple arrived in Pittsburgh, where Lucy was able to recover during their two weeks of waiting for a flatboat with space for passengers and goods. Pittsburgh was a raw, grimy town booming with business, but their stay there was as much as a honeymoon as they would get.

Finally, they got passage on a flatboat, a large rectangular raft-like boat, carried along in the river current. Packing their own food and bedding, the newlyweds had to claim their personal space among the crew and other passengers, pigs, goats, sheep, cows, and horses as well as farm equipment and carriages.

Louisville

After arriving in Louisville in early May, they settled in a hotel and were content with their new location. Lucy adjusted well to the gentry of Louisville. "My young wife, who possessed talents far above par, was regarded as a gem, and received by them all with the greatest pleasure," John wrote.

One of his new drawings, created in early July, was of a belted kingfisher, the same species he had depicted after positioning a freshly killed specimen in a lifelike pose using wire. Using pastel, graphite, and ink, he created a vibrant portrait of a very alert-looking female in profile, its eye staring directly at the viewer. Also in the picture are delicate renditions of a wing and tail feather. It is easy for viewers to see he was developing his skill.

"The quills, which I used for drawing feet and claws of so many small birds were so hard and yet so elastic that the best steel pen of present day might have blushed if it could be compared with them," he wrote.

Among the prominent citizens of Louisville were various members of the Clark family, related

Flatboat with passengers and cargo.
Historic New Orleans Collection, WikiCommons

to William Clark, coleader of the Lewis and Clark expedition that explored the western portion of the Louisiana Purchase from 1803 to 1806.

William's eldest brother was General Jonathan Clark, and the second oldest brother, General George Rogers Clark, was a Revolutionary War hero who had captured a British Fort with only a small band of frontiersmen. Since he had helped to establish the first Anglo-American settlement at the site of the current city in 1778 during the Revolutionary War, he was nicknamed "the father of Louisville." Their sister Lucy was married to William Croghan, a major in George Washington's army, who had known Captain Audubon during the war.

John James Audubon became close friends with the Croghan's son George, whose uncle General William Clark, now governor of the Louisiana Territory, would sometimes visit from St. Louis, headquarters of his militia. Two other Louisville families, the Tarascons and Berthouds, both French and living upriver in Shippingport, welcomed Lucy.

By early June, Audubon was adding to his growing number of bird pictures. Two of them were of orchard orioles he had observed downriver from Louisville. An orchard oriole builds a nest suspended from tree branches, and several pairs may build a nest in the same or adjacent trees.

"The nest is of a hemispherical form, and is supported by the margin only. It seldom exceeds three or four inches in depth, is open almost to the full extent of its largest diameter at the top or entrance, and finished on all sides, as well as

(above) **Belted kingfisher.**
Houghton Library, Harvard University, WikiCommons

(left) **Orchard orioles with nest.**

Bird Zippers

A bird's wings are made up of feathers specialized for flight, called remiges, with windproof surfaces, or vanes, on either side of the central shaft. These feathers are asymmetric with a shorter, less flexible leading edge that prevents midair twisting. These large, stiff feathers have a quill that attaches to the wing bones. The wing bones correspond to the three bones in our arms. At the tip are the hand bones, which bear the longer vaned feathers known as primaries. Below the wrist, other shorter vaned feathers called secondaries are attached to the forearm and upper arm. At the base of primary and secondary feathers are rows of smaller feathers, known as coverts, that cover quills.

Birds shed old worn feathers and then grow new ones. This is known as molting. Birds molt to replace worn flight feathers and to change winter seasonal plumage for breeding. You will use these molted feathers in this activity.

YOU WILL NEED:

- ↯ Feathers found in the wild
- ↯ Bird-Watching Journal
- ↯ Pen or pencil
- ↯ Magnifying lens (optional)

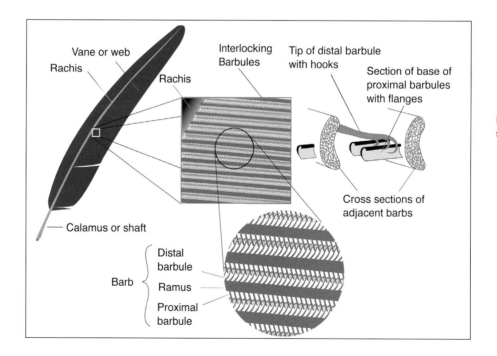

Diagram of a feather's structure. *WikiCommons*

Keep on the lookout for feathers that have fallen to the ground. Other sources of feathers: pet birds that friends or neighbors may have, pet stores that sell birds, local poultry farms, or seashores or lakeshores with numerous water birds.

First, note the shape of the two feathers in Audubon's painting of the kingfishers (page 17). The upper feather narrows to a pointed tip and narrows to the shaft at the base. Old wing feathers are worn on the side that is most abraded by the air. Tail feathers, like the lower one in the picture, have an oblong shape.

Carefully observe the feathers you have found and use a magnifying lens if one is available. A flight feather is like a tree. It has a main trunk, called a shaft, branches, called barbs, and smaller side branches called barbules. The barbs on the wing or tail feather have microscopic hooks on the barbules. The barbs are so well locked together that each wing feather is extremely strong, and the way the wing and tail feathers overlap allows the tail and wing to resist tremendous air pressure.

Hold the feather by the bottom of the shaft and fan it in front of your face. Run your fingers down the barbs of a tail or wing feather so that the barbs separate. Now fan your face with the feather again. Can you feel a difference in the amount of air pushed into your face?

Now run your fingers back up the feather several times, flattening it out. Notice how the air space between the barbs has disappeared. Record what you learned in your Bird-Watching Journal.

Felsentaube
(Columba livia f. dom.)
190 mm - H6

Waldohreule
(Asio otus)
240 mm - H7

Saatkrähe
(Corvus frugilegus)
233 mm - H4

Worn wing feathers (from left to right): rock dove, long eared owl, and rook. *WikiCommons*

within, with the long slender grasses . . . Some of these go round the nest several times, as if coarsely woven together," observed Audubon.

At the end of July, Major Croghan told Audubon about a massive sycamore tree where chimney swifts came to roost (Audubon called them chimney swallows). Audubon returned home and then went back to the tree at dusk to witness the swifts coming back to the roost. "The sun was going down behind the Silver Hills; the evening was beautiful; thousands of Swallows were flying above me, and three or four at a time were pitching into the hole (in a branch stub 40 feet [12.1 m] above)."

When he pressed his ear against the hollow tree trunk, he heard a roaring noise inside. The next morning at dawn he witnessed the birds pour out of the tree in a continuous black stream. He estimated that 9,000 birds roosted inside this single tree.

When birds roost together, it is like an enormous slumber party where they all go to sleep in the same place. Roosting sites provide birds with a safe place to rest or sleep. In winter, roosts keep birds warmer by blocking the wind and lessening the cold. Through huddling, birds can increase their body heat. Sleeping in a roost in a large cavity is safer than sleeping out in the open.

Birds normally sleep sitting up with the head and neck resting on the back and the bill buried in the shoulder feathers. This posture allows their necks to relax and their eyes to be protected from the cold.

A Growing Family

By late fall, Lucy was pregnant with their first child. John James and Ferdinand's business had slowed down along with other business due to trade issues with Europe.

In May 1809, in Lucy's eighth month of pregnancy, John James made the long voyage to Mill Grove to investigate the sale of the property. When he returned home, he joined a swan-hunting expedition hundreds of miles downriver. He made it back to Louisville just in time to be with his wife for the birth of Victor Gifford Audubon on June 12, 1809.

In March 1810, a formally dressed Scotsman, carrying two large books under his arm, entered Audubon and Rozier's store. His name was Alexander Wilson, and the books were the first two volumes of his *American Ornithology*. He was seeking funds to publish further volumes. He did this by asking for subscriptions, essentially advanced payment, for the entire set. Wilson had met Lucy's uncle, Benjamin Bakewell, who recommended visiting John James in Louisville.

When John James looked at Wilson's first two volumes of *American Ornithology*, he immediately wanted to subscribe. He was excited about all the information Wilson had collected, but also clearly realized that his own drawings of American birds were superior to Wilson's. Rozier interrupted in French and told Audubon that not only did they not have the money to subscribe, but that Audubon's artwork was better.

When Wilson got a look at Audubon's watercolors, he was crestfallen. These pictures by this young Frenchman in a frontier town were far better than Wilson's. Graciously, Audubon offered to take Wilson on outings to see some bird species not mentioned in his books, like whooping cranes nesting on nearby ponds.

Later in May, Audubon and Rozier's property at Mill Grove sold for a value equivalent to $150,000 in 2021. Business in Louisville was still not as good as they wished due to too many competitors. Audubon wanted to move farther south for wilder land to explore, and Rozier wanted more profit. Henderson, an outpost 125 miles (201 km) down the Ohio River, offered both.

Chimney swifts.

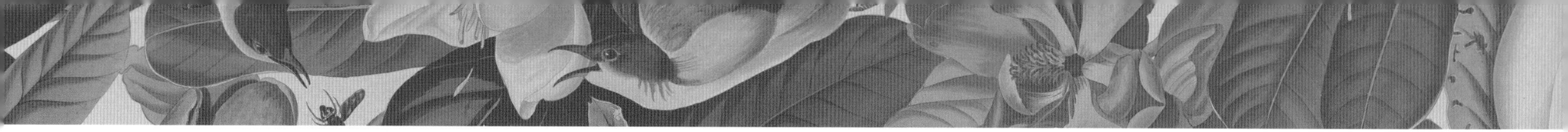

Eggamination

Consider the term "egg shaped." All eggs, whether large or small, have a similar shape. They are roundish, but not round. They are ellipsoidal, which means they are longer than wide, a shape that makes them stronger and roomier than if they were spheroid (round). Their shape also makes it less likely that an egg will roll away like a ball.

Inside, eggs are the familiar yolk and egg white (albumen). The embryo develops within the yolk; it gets its food from the yolk and the egg white. The egg is like a space capsule with almost everything the developing chick needs, except a bit of fresh air.

Just inside an egg's shell are two membranes. When inside the mother bird, the egg is very warm, but once it is laid, it cools off, causing the two membranes to separate enough to form a small pocket or sack of air. As the bird developing inside the egg grows, it breathes in oxygen from this sack and exhales carbon dioxide.

Several thousand microscopic pores are found all over the surface of the egg that allow the CO_2 to escape and fresh air to get in. The ellipsoidal shape provides a greater surface area for pores.

YOU WILL NEED:

↘ Chicken egg

↘ Small bowl

↘ Bird-Watching Journal

↘ Pen or pencil

Place a chicken egg on the floor and try to roll it. What happens?

The next time you or a parent cracks an egg to cook, break it into a bowl first. Look at the yolk and the egg white. What do you observe about the egg when you look at it closely?

Examine the curve of the shell. The curve makes it easier for a hatching chick to crack the shell open. Are you able to take a close look at the membrane? Record all your observations in your Bird-Watching Journal.

Nat Pope, the clerk from their Louisville store, accompanied them to Henderson, where John James and Lucy moved into an abandoned log cabin. They filled the drafty gaps between the logs and spread bearskins over the hard dirt floor. Now they were truly living like settlers on the frontier.

Lucy was delighted when she and John James were befriended by a physician named Adam Rankin and his educated wife Elizabeth Rankin, who lived in a large log house, called Meadowbrook, just outside of town. Elizabeth became a new friend.

Audubon's attire changed as well. Gone were his fancy waistcoats and breeches. He now wore a hunting shirt and pants made of deer hide. On his feet were moccasins, and in his belt, he carried a ball pouch, a buffalo horn full of gunpowder, a large hunting knife, and a tomahawk. He and Pope provided meat and fish for the table, while Rozier managed the store.

Rozier was disappointed in their slow business. His English was not very good, and he missed being around French people, so he decided to move to St. Genevieve, a French settlement on the banks of the Mississippi River. Audubon wanted to "take a measure" of the place first, before he decided to move from Henderson, but agreed to help Rozier transport merchandise for the new business venture. They loaded up a flatboat with barrels of whiskey, gunpowder, and other goods to sell once they got there.

The Rankins had invited Lucy and young Victor to stay with them while John James was away and asked Lucy to teach the Rankin children. It

WHY BIRDS DON'T GET PREGNANT AND OTHER ADAPTATIONS FOR FLIGHT

If you wished to fly like a bird, your body would have to weigh less. Instead of having a heavy jaw and teeth for chewing, you would need a light beak. Rather than keeping warm with a heavy wool or fur coat, you would need a lightweight down jacket. And for females, instead of being pregnant with an embryo developing and growing inside your body, you would lay eggs and then incubate them until they hatched.

The Rankin house may have looked like this Tennessee log home from the same period. *WikiCommons*

Bird Bills

Audubon often heard or saw ivory-billed woodpeckers in nearby old-growth forests. With a wingspan of two and a half feet (76 cm), this is the largest of woodpeckers in the United States. Their long white bills act like chisels as they hack into trees hunting for large beetle grubs, some over an inch long. "When taken by the hand, which is a rather hazardous undertaking, they strike with great violence, and inflict very severe wounds with their bills as well as claws," wrote Audubon.

Bird bills come in all shapes and sizes. The tip of the bill on a red crossbill crosses when closed but when open works like forceps as it pulls seeds from conifer cones. A finch's viselike bill is a perfect seed cruncher.

● ●

YOU WILL NEED:

↘ Pen or pencil

↘ Bird-Watching Journal

↘ Pen or pencil

↘ Binoculars

Examine a variety of bird bills carefully through binoculars and sketch them in your Bird-Watching Journal. Be sure to show the shape and size. See if you can sketch the bills of three to five local birds.

Compare each bill's length to the width of the bird's head. Downy woodpeckers are smaller than hairy woodpeckers, but if you don't have both species visible at the same time, you can tell them apart by looking at the length of their bills. The bill of a downy woodpecker is a little more than a quarter of the width of its head, while that of the hairy woodpecker is almost one half the width of its head.

was a relief for John James that his family was in good hands, as the flatboat floated off from Henderson a few days before Christmas.

Near the mouth of the Ohio River, their way was blocked by ice on the Mississippi River close to an encampment of Shawnee who were gathering pecans and hunting. John James joined the Shawnee on their hunts. Learning of his interest in birds and other animals, they offered to help collect and trap specimens in exchange for knives, scissors, and other desired tools, and shared knowledge of the local birds. There, 100 miles (161 km) downriver from St. Genevieve, they waited until the spring thaw.

Once the ice broke up enough for them to travel up the Mississippi River, it took more than two months to reach St. Genevieve. On their way, about six miles (9.6 km) below the confluence of the Ohio and Mississippi Rivers, Audubon encountered thousands of Carolina parakeets roosting in large sycamore trees. He carefully described their colors: "Forepart of the head and the cheeks bright scarlet, that colour extending over and behind the eye, the rest of the head and the neck pure bright yellow; the edge of the wing bright yellow, spotted with orange. The general colour of the other parts is emerald-green, with light blue reflections, lighter beneath. Primary coverts deep bluish-green; secondary coverts greenish-yellow."

The Carolina parakeet is one of many species Audubon depicted that is now extinct due to overhunting.

Rozier was pleased with St. Genevieve, but Audubon found it "small and dirty." After years of

· · · · · ·

Describe the Colors and Patterns of a Common Neighborhood Bird

Select a common wild bird from your neighborhood. Study the diagram of the names of a bird's body parts below, then write down the colors of your bird's parts in your Bird-Watching Journal.

Bird topography.
Illustration by Jim Spence

being partners, Audubon negotiated a sale of his stake in the business, and the two parted ways.

To get back home to Henderson, Audubon had to walk 125 miles (201 km) across Illinois Territory. Remarkably it only took three days, despite the lack of traction his smooth-soled moccasins had. He arrived at the Rankins a few days before his 26th birthday, happy to be back with Lucy and Victor.

By May he was back to his drawing and considered his next business venture. Lucy's brother Tom had written that he was coming for a visit. In midsummer the Audubons moved to the Indian Queen Hotel in Louisville. It was a hot, dry summer that led to crop failures. Lucy and John James survived the heat by swimming, sometimes across the Ohio River.

Tom Bakewell arrived in September with the news that he was on his way to New Orleans to start a business importing goods from Liverpool, England, and exporting cotton from New Orleans. Needing his French language skills, he wanted Audubon to be his partner.

Lucy was thrilled by the idea of her husband and brother being partners, but it would take time. Tom left for New Orleans, and John James traveled back to St. Genevieve by foot to collect money owed him by Rozier. When he returned empty-handed, he and Lucy decided to visit her father at Fatland Ford, to get funds from him and so he could finally meet his grandson, Victor, now two years old. They set off on horseback, with Victor riding in a basket tied to the saddle horn in front of his father.

The cold November weather made the 800-mile (1,287-km) journey more challenging, especially when they had to ford a frigid river. In Pittsburgh they warmed up and recovered their strength for four days with Lucy's aunt and uncle before resuming their trip. Lucy commented that the roads were still "really dreadful" and scattered with "rocks and stumps or roots of trees." Lucy was exhibiting a toughness that well matched that of her husband.

The family arrived at Fatland Ford just before December. They were ecstatic to be reunited with her sisters, little brother, and father, but her step-mother's unfriendliness cast a shadow on the visit. Audubon took off on horseback for New Orleans via Henderson to join up with Tom.

On January 23, 1812, while riding through the prairies in central Kentucky, he heard a distant rumbling, and his horse slowed to a walk, placing its hooves with care "as if walking on a smooth sheet of ice." Groaning, it spread its legs to brace itself as the whole earth underneath them shook. This was one of many aftershocks from a massive earthquake that had occurred in mid-December centered near the town of New Madrid in Missouri Territory. The quake had been felt from Canada to the Gulf of Mexico and from the Rocky Mountains to the Atlantic coast.

Back in Henderson, Audubon retrieved a wooden chest left in the care of friends that contained 200 bird drawings, that when added to previous work would make 1,000. But to his horror he discovered Norway rats had used the paper to make a nest. He was devastated.

"The burning heat that rushed through my brain was too great to be endured, affecting my whole nervous system," Audubon wrote in his journal. It was if he had been kicked in the stomach. The hours and hours he had labored painting was all for naught. Most of the work had been created in spare moments between his hours running the store. He could not sleep or focus on anything else until, as he described, "My animal powers were called back into action through the strength of my constitution."

He once again set off into the woods with his gun, notebook, and pencil "gaily, as if nothing had happened." It took him three years to redo those lost drawings, but they were all of better quality in the end.

Starting Over

Audubon got news from Tom Bakewell that the coming war with England would doom any business venture. Audubon returned to Fatland Ford by early spring, happy to be reunited with his family. He set to work, adding to his portfolio of bird portraits, including a spotted sandpiper.

Shortly after his 27th birthday, Audubon had a breakthrough. His art training had not included learning a technique called foreshortening, a method for drawing objects that makes them appear to come off the page. It is often used in comic books and graphic novels. By trial and error, he had figured out how to create this illusion as shown by his drawing of a whip-poor-will in flight. This was a step that would set his bird

Whip-poor-wills.

Describing Flight

Bird flight is as varied as birds themselves. Fowl such as quail are slow, heavy fliers. Hawks and vultures use their large wings to spiral upward on air drafts. Hummingbirds can hover and fly backward, while swallows gracefully swoop through the open sky. Some birds such as penguins, kiwis, and ostriches, have wings but have lost the ability to fly.

John James Audubon was a careful observer and detailed writer. He used a wide variety of words to describe bird flight. Below is a list of words from his *Birds of America*:

Glide, soar, powerful, swift, undulate, sail, flapping, sweep, sluggish, steady, quick, graceful, darting, dashing, pitch, plummet, whirling, whirring, elegant, gyrate.

In describing a bird's flight, you can compare it to jets, kites, rockets, and any other things that fly. Does it flap continuously or flap and glide? Does it fly directly to a perch or feeding spot? As you observe neighborhood birds, take note of patterns in flight in your Bird-Watching Journal.

painting apart from the rigid illustrations of earlier bird artists, which were stiff but accurate in terms of actual measurements.

Instead of opening a business with Audubon in New Orleans, Tom joined Audubon in Henderson to reopen the general store. In Henderson new farms were producing high yields of both corn and tobacco, and the population was growing. The store attracted many customers, and by the time the Audubons' second son John Woodhouse was born on November 30, 1812, they were back on their feet.

Now Lucy and John James had enough money to buy a one-and-a-half-story log home with a large front porch, next to the store. On the property was also a stable, a smokehouse, a springhouse for keeping food cool, and an orchard.

One autumn while crossing barrens, as prairies were then called, Audubon witnessed passenger pigeons flying in greater numbers than he had ever seen before. When a hawk approached the rear of one flock to hunt, Audubon was amazed by their response.

"All at once—like a torrent—and with the noise of thunder—they rushed together to form a compact mass. The pigeons darted forward in undulating and angular lines, descended and swept close over the earth with inconceivable velocity."

That winter Audubon began investing in real estate in Henderson, where the price of lots was expected to increase. In January 1814 he opened another store 60 miles (97 km) downriver in Shawneetown, Illinois Territory. The manager of the store agreed to divide the profits with Audubon and Bakewell.

Now Lucy and Tom were prosperous citizens in the quickly growing town of Henderson. As his father had, John James purchased slaves to work in the house, their property, and store. At one time, Audubon wrote, "To repay evil with kindness is the religion that I was taught to practice, and this will forever be my rule." But by owning slaves, which many people considered an evil act, Audubon was an evildoer. While these slaves labored for them, John James and Lucy enjoyed leisure activities such as horseback rides, swimming, and long walks. John James competed in horse races, often coming in first. He excelled in shooting competitions and was known for his prowess as a sword fighter.

Bakewell had the idea to build a mill on the Ohio River for milling both lumber and flour. It seemed like a good idea that would earn them a profit.

With a large house, Lucy was able to invite her younger sister Eliza and brother William to come live with them. They wanted to get away from the mistreatment by their stepmother. They arrived in November 1814, one month before Lucy's third child was due.

4

LOSSES AND SUCCESSES

···········

The Audubons' third child Lucy was born in December 1814. Tragically, the baby had a condition called hydrocephalus. In the brain are
fluids that bathe brain tissue. When excess fluid builds up in the brain
cavity, damage to the brain can occur. Today, babies born with hydrocephalus can have an operation to help drain excess fluid, but in the early

Mallard ducks.

Passenger pigeons.

19th century there was no successful treatment for the condition. Baby Lucy lived only two years.

The death of Lucy was the beginning of a series of great losses for the Audubon family. Nationally, the economy was faltering. Over the next few years, the earnings from their stores would plummet, but it was their investment in a mill that would doom them.

Tom married the daughter of one of his uncle Benjamin's business associates in Pittsburgh during the summer of 1815, and they soon moved to Henderson. It didn't take long for his bride, Elizabeth, to dislike the small frontier town and demand that they move back to Pittsburgh. Though the mill had been his idea, Tom followed his wife's wish, and John James lost his partner. The cost of the mill kept going up.

The year 1816, the same year baby Lucy died, was known as the year without summer. A massive volcanic explosion of Mount Tambora in the Dutch East Indies (Indonesia) in April of the previous year sent ash around the world. So much ash and gases were added to the atmosphere that it acted like a blanket blocking the sun. The resulting cold temperatures caused frost and snow during summer months in the northern hemisphere. Crops failed, causing food shortages and even famine.

In Kentucky people were hungry. Migrating passenger pigeons roosted in inconceivable numbers. The weight of these roosting pigeons broke tree limbs. Pigeon dung, inches thick, covered the forest floor. During the summer Audubon observed one roost that was 40 miles (64 km) long and 3 miles (4.8 km) wide. When he arrived at it two hours before sunset, when the pigeons were returning to roost, a great number of people with wagons and guns were there. After dark descended, all waited in silence until they heard what sounded like a gale-force wind. Then the guns started blasting, and pigeons fell in thousands. This was food for people who might have otherwise starved. Audubon and his young brother-in-law filled four large sacks full of dead pigeons to feed their large household.

Both the grist mill and sawmill were finished, but there weren't enough farmers growing wheat to provide customers for the grist mill, and there was not enough demand for lumber. It was a poorly conceived and executed venture, and Audubon was the one now responsible for it. To cover debts from its construction, he sold off land, and the family moved to a smaller house. But that wasn't enough. To make matters worse, woodcutters he had hired to get timber for the mill never cut any trees and stole his axes and oxen.

"Up went the mill at an enormous expense in a country unfit for such a thing as it would now be for me to attempt to settle on the moon," wrote Audubon. He also commented, "Of all the follies of man, the building of that accursed mill was one of the greatest."

Constantine Rafinesque

One day in late summer, as John James was walking along the riverbank, he sighted an odd-looking man dressed in a long, loose, well-worn yellow coat, a long waistcoat with enormous pockets jammed full of plants, and pantaloons buttoned to his shoes. His long hair and beard gave him the look of a vagabond. He approached Audubon and asked if he knew a Mr. Audubon. Audubon warmly greeted him as he was shown a letter of introduction from friends describing him as an odd fish.

Thus Audubon came to know Constantine Rafinesque. An eccentric genius, Rafinesque had read 1,000 books by age 12, authored his first scientific paper at 13, and spoke six languages. Audubon recounted that he had stopped at Henderson "expressly for the purpose of seeing my drawings."

While viewing the drawings, Rafinesque noticed a plant he thought was new to science. He demanded that Audubon show him where it grew.

Along the Ohio River and other rivers, including the Mississippi, were dense growths of giant cane, a native bamboo. Canebrakes vegetated riversides ravaged by floods, stabilizing the banks and providing habitat for many bird species.

Audubon tired out his guest by pushing backward through dense canebrakes, suffering scratches from brambles and stings from nettles, and having a close encounter with a startled bear.

But when they found the plant, Rafinesque became overjoyed and said it was not only a new species, but a new genus. Audubon realized the man was obsessed with discovering new species.

Possibly annoyed at his guest's fixation with "discoveries," Audubon drew a picture of a fish called a devil-jack diamond fish that he claimed to have seen in the Ohio River, which grew as long as 10 feet (3 m) and was bulletproof. This tall tale, intended as a joke, was taken seriously by Rafinesque, who made a sketch of it in his notebook. Of course, no such fish existed, but when Rafinesque published his book on American fish years later, it included this fictional species.

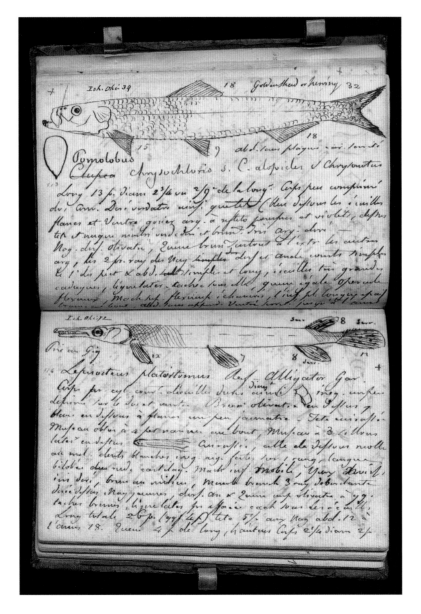

One night the Audubons were awakened by noise coming from upstairs where Rafinesque was sleeping. Upon investigating, John James discovered the naked naturalist running about the room trying to kill bats with John James's violin, severely damaging it. Rafinesque claimed they were likely a new species. After a three-week stay, their guest was gone one morning with no word of farewell.

Further Losses

Audubon was hurt further by both personal and business losses. Audubon's father, Jean Audubon, died in February 1818. John James had not seen his father in over ten years.

The next year, Audubon and other merchants throughout the nation were walloped by a financial crisis called the Panic of 1819, or the first great depression. As banks struggled to stay open, their banknotes became almost worthless. Audubon was unable to pay off loans for the mill and bills for goods he sold. Profits from his stores had dwindled. In June he gave up his store to creditors and a month later sold his portion of the mill, all his slaves, and his woodlot. He sold their house and land and possessions. All he had left were the clothes on his back, his drawings, and gun.

Despite selling everything, he still did not have enough money to pay off his debts. He left Lucy, soon to give birth to a fourth child, and the boys in Henderson with friends and headed for Louisville to find work. Upon his arrival there, he was thrown in jail for not paying his debts. With the help of friends he was released and joined Lucy and the boys at her sister's home just up the river in Shippingport. Not long after, daughter Rose was born.

Audubon later wrote in his journal about these hard times: "One of the most extraordinary things among all these adverse circumstances was that I never for a day gave up listening to the songs of our birds, or watching their peculiar habits, or delineating them in the best way that I could; nay, during my deepest troubles I frequently would wrench myself from the persons around me, and retire to some secluded part of our noble forests; and many a time, at the sound of the wood-thrush's melodies have I fallen on my knees, and there prayed earnestly to our God."

Art to the Rescue

"Nothing was left to me but my humble talents."
—*John James Audubon*

As brother-in-law William Bakewell wrote in his memoirs, the world owed a debt of gratitude to the "infernal" mill for forcing Audubon to pursue his talent for depicting birds through art and writing. During the last years in Henderson, he had spent little time following his passion for rambling and drawing. Now he had no choice. The loss of his retail business had left him humiliated. Though his next venture would take time and require great strength, from both him and Lucy, they would be rewarded.

Without a penny in his pocket, Audubon's next step was drawing portraits for $5 apiece (roughly $110 in 2022). He felt that due to his misfortune, his skill at drawing birds had improved.

Meanwhile, the Audubons depended on the hospitality of Lucy's sister Eliza, who had once lived with them and was now married to Audubon's friend Nicholas Berthoud. Eliza gave birth to a baby girl that autumn. At the time, baby Rose was sickly and weak. And in yet one more tragic event for Lucy and John James, the baby died at seven months of age.

Friends blamed John James for his family's circumstances. They said his love for socializing and wandering in the wilds caused his loss of everything. Ironically, during the years previous to his bankruptcy, he had spent most of his time dealing with the mill and store and neglected his exploring and drawing of bird life.

Through a friend, Audubon was hired for a job preparing birds for exhibits at the newly established Western Museum of Cincinnati College in Ohio. The salary offered was a very generous $125 a month. While he worked there, "the expedition of Major Long passed through the city," and they visited the museum. The museum director showed them Audubon's artwork, "and well do I recollect how he [Major Long], Messrs. T, Peale, Thomas Say and others stared at my drawings." This interest from prominent artist Titian Peale and naturalist Thomas Say boosted his confidence, as did praise by museum patrons.

One of his latest compositions was of a new species he discovered across the Ohio River in Kentucky that he later named Henslow's bunting (now Henslow's sparrow). This was one of many species he would name after friends. "I never saw this species alight on trees, but on the ground, where it spends its time; it runs with rapidity, passing through the grass with the swiftness of a mouse."

We recognize people we know from a distance by their posture, their distinctive walk, and distinct behaviors, such as tilting their head, putting their hands on their hips, or moving their body side to side when not walking. We are able to do this without consciously thinking, *That's Lucy because she tosses her hair or swings her arms.* We recognize birds in a similar way. For example, thrushes such as robins and bluebirds hold their body at a 45-degree angle while resting.

Wood thrush.

Lucy and the children had joined John James and they lived frugally in a small house. The promised salary was never paid due to the museum's poor finances. Audubon worked diligently preparing exhibits, but after six months he was dismissed with the promise of receiving his pay in the future.

Audubon hunted and fished to put food on the table and started a drawing school to earn money for rent. One student, Joseph Mason, had exceptional skills as both an artist and a botanist. Even with all his duties, Audubon made time for collecting bird specimens for drawings that not only were improving in quality but also growing in quantity.

"Having a tolerably large number of drawings that have been greatly admired, I concluded I could not do better than to travel and finish my collection or so nearly that it would become a valuable acquisition," he recalled. "My wife hoped that it might do well."

Since she had first met John James, Lucy was fascinated by his interest in birds and was proud of his skill at depicting them. She encouraged his goal of creating a book of North American birds with illustrations of each bird in lifelike action. Despite the hardship of caring for her sons by herself, as well as running a small school to pay for food and lodging, she knew that her husband needed to explore. She was not a complainer. No matter what her family said, she had faith in her husband's talents and ambition. As he received more critical praise, such as the review of an exhibition of his art at the Western Museum, the success of his project grew more certain.

In winter 1820, the *Cincinnati Inquisitor Advertiser* wrote, "The style & execution of these paintings . . . are so very superior, that we believe we hazard nothing in saying, there have been no exhibitions west of the mountains which can compare with them. Good judges have indeed declared they excel all other similar works in the United States."

Audubon loved to watch cliff swallows and would observe and sketch them at a nesting colony across the Ohio River in Kentucky. For centuries, naturalists explained the absence of swallows in winter by proposing that they simply buried themselves in mud until spring.

Audubon questioned this idea. "Being extremely desirous of settling the long-agitated question respecting the migration or supposed torpidity of Swallows, I embraced every opportunity of examining their habits, carefully noted their arrival and disappearance, and recorded every fact connected with their history," he later wrote.

Through his observations of swallows, warblers, and thrushes in different places and seasons, he determined that these birds were migratory. Other species such as chickadees and northern cardinals are called all-year residents because they rarely migrate.

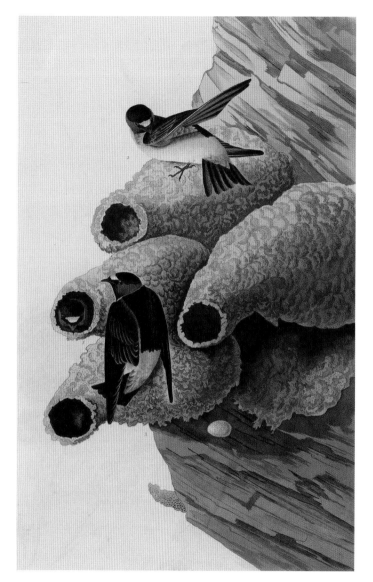

Cliff swallows.

Down the River

Now that he had no work with the museum and his art was being praised, Audubon was more determined than ever to pursue his grand project of picturing and writing about the birds of

America. His plan was to float down the Ohio and Mississippi Rivers to explore the delta and gulf before traveling to Florida and back up the eastern coast.

Lucy would stay behind in Cincinnati with Victor, now 11, and John Woodhouse, now 8, as she waited for money owed her husband by the Western Museum. She would live off tuition paid by students at her small private school and money that Audubon was earning from teaching and painting portraits. He would take off on his long journey with not a penny in his pocket: "Without any money My talents are to be my support and my anthusiasm (enthusiasm) My guide in my difficulties."

Audubon planned to eliminate the cost of boat fare by finding a flatboat captain who would provide passage in exchange for wild game that Audubon killed for food for the passengers and crew. After approaching one captain after another

BIRD MIGRATION

Many bird species breed in northern locales and winter in the south. Canada warblers nest in the Northeast and Midwest of the United States and also in Canada. For winter they travel to northern South America. Insects and spiders that are their main food are abundant in the north in summer, so there is plenty to feed their quickly growing nestlings.

House wren parents have been observed making 1,000 trips a day, delivering food to older nestlings. In each trip they bring an average of ten insects or spiders back to the nest. One thousand trips multiplied by 10 equals 10,000 "bugs." Between both parents, they may collect 20,000 "bugs" per day. As northern days shorten and plants lose leaves or die, the number of "bugs" decreases rapidly. There still will be enough to supply chickadees, nuthatches, and other wintering birds that are extremely adept at searching out "bugs" for food. Other species, however, travel south where there is a steady supply of food year-round.

A lot of people assume that birds fly south in winter because it gets too cold for them. But a bird's down feathers provide plenty of insulation to keep it warm. Yet without enough food, a bird must leave for regions richer with winter food.

JOURNALING

••••••

Describe the Unique Behavior of Neighborhood Birds

Sit in a comfortable place where you often see birds and watch individual birds as they go about their day. Examine how they move, search for food, and interact with other birds. Take notes on what you notice in your Bird-Watching Journal. If you wish, sketch their stance or other aspects of their behavior. Writing about what we observe makes us more aware of the world around us and helps us the realize what we are really seeing.

he finally found one, Jacob Aumack, captain of a large flatboat, who agreed to the deal. Accompanying Audubon was his 13-year-old student Joseph Mason, who would draw plants for Audubon's compositions.

Leaving his family for what was supposed to be a 7-month journey, but would last 14 instead, was heart-wrenching for John James. He worried about Lucy and the boys' ability to get by, and Lucy's sadness made it all that much harder. However, she had encouraged him, as she always did, and he had great faith in his own power to succeed.

At 4:30 PM on October 12, 1820, John James Audubon and Joseph Mason began their journey aboard Aumack's flatboat. His luggage was limited to paper, pencils, crayons, chalk, a scoring board, a roll of wire used for positioning his birds in lifelike poses, a copy of Turton's *Linnaeus* for use in bird identification, and a new journal for his notes. He also brought his rifle and ammunition, violin, and flute.

On his first day serving as the flatboat's official hunter, he killed 30 partridge and 27 grey squirrels, and Mason shot 3 turkeys. Each time that he went ashore to hunt he would also shoot specimens for drawing. His goal was to draw a new species each day, but it often took longer. Some days when they floated all day long, he drew hour after hour, as well as kept up on his journal writing.

They saw large flocks of snow geese, chimney swifts, and other birds flying south for winter. As they passed Louisville and neared Henderson, Audubon had no interest in visiting his old home but wanted his hunting dog Dash that he had

Keep Track of Neighborhood Birds Through the Year

Swallow, swifts, orioles, and tanagers are all birds that summer in the north and winter in the tropics or subtropics. If you live in the far south, many of your neighborhood birds will leave for the north in early spring and return in autumn. If you live in the north, the migration pattern will be reversed, with some birds leaving in autumn and returning in the spring.

This activity will take some time, as you will record your observations over the course of a year (or more).

• •

YOU WILL NEED:

↘ Bird-Watching Journal
↘ Pen or pencil

Keep track of each species of bird you identify in your neighborhood. Always write the date you spotted the bird.

After a year of recording observations, you will be able to more easily determine which species leave and which are around all year. Of those that leave, you'll know when they leave, in late summer or mid-autumn, and you'll note when migrants return in the spring.

In the early 1800s the region of Missouri and Tennessee along the Mississippi River was covered by massive swamps.

I wish, kind reader, it were in my power to present to your mind's eye the favourite resort of the Ivory-billed Woodpecker. Would that I could describe the extent of those deep morasses, overshadowed by millions of gigantic dark cypresses, spreading their sturdy moss-covered branches, as if to admonish intruding man to pause and reflect on the many difficulties which he must encounter, should he persist in venturing farther into their almost inaccessible recesses, extending for miles before him, where he should be interrupted by huge projecting branches, here and there the massy trunk of a fallen and decaying tree, and thousands of creeping and twining plants of numberless species!

In his journal, Audubon noted that the ivory-billed woodpeckers were always seen in pairs. Like many woodpecker species, the males and females were sexually dimorphic, meaning they had distinctly different appearances. Males had a red patch on the back of the head; females did not.

Continuing down the river, Audubon and Mason passed the grand Chickasaw Bluffs colored with layers of red, yellow, and black, all riddled with thousands of bank swallow nesting holes. It was raining too hard for Audubon to sketch them. Two days later, on December 1, he heard a loud noise overhead. At first, he thought it might be winds at the head of a storm, but soon he realized

left there with a friend. Mason and a friend went ashore and brought back the retriever.

On November 24, about 25 miles (40 km) downstream from New Madrid, Missouri, Audubon sighted ivory-billed woodpeckers in the swamp forests along the shore where they were pecking holes in old-growth bald cypress trees for large beetle grubs.

it came from the wingbeats of large flocks of mergansers flying south. Two days later he shot two female mergansers, which he closely examined before drawing.

They were now just north of Natchez, Mississippi, with the state of Mississippi on the eastern bank and the state of Louisiana on the western bank. Audubon was entering a new region with unique bird species found in the southern United States, Caribbean, and Mexico.

On Christmas, he thought of Lucy and the boys, wishing he was with them. His mood was brightened by the gift of a great-footed hawk (peregrine falcon). "I have often seen them after hearing their Canon Ball like wistling Noise through the Air sieze their prey on the Wing," he wrote, and now he had one in hand to draw.

The following day they docked at Natchez. Mississippi, just before noon. Audubon unexpectedly ran into his brother-in-law Nicholas Berthoud, who was also on his way to New Orleans. Berthoud graciously offered Audubon and Mason passage on his keelboat. Audubon gladly accepted. This would be a faster and more comfortable ride the remainder of their trip.

Within four days, with the assistance of Berthoud's servants, Mason and Audubon transferred their possessions from Captain Aumack's flatboat to Berthoud's keelboat. Audubon routinely called slaves servants, perhaps to minimize the inhumanity of slaveholders like himself.

Leaving the servants to load everything aboard the keelboat proved to be a mistake. It wasn't until after they departed that Audubon discovered a

Mama and Papa Pairs

Can you find male and female birds with different appearances? With some familiar birds, such as the mallard, the male, with its glossy green neck and head, and the female, with its brown speckled body, are easily told apart. With other species, like American robins, the difference between males and females is more subtle. The male has a darker orange-red breast and darker black head than the female, who is drab in comparison.

YOU WILL NEED:

- Bird field guide for your region (western, eastern)
- Binoculars
- Bird-Watching Journal
- Pen or pencil

Examine your neighborhood birds to see if any are in pairs.

Using a field guide, determine the difference, if any, between males and females. Record your observations in your Bird-Watching Journal. How many different pairs did you find?

In this robin family, the male robin is directly feeding the two nestlings; you can tell which is the male by its rich orange breast. The female, dull in comparison, is perched higher in the nest and holds a seed in its beak.

and thrushes and the river with water birds. During his last week on the river, Audubon delighted in the birds he saw and drew, despite the discomfort of stormy weather, including snow.

"If this is not the winter retreat of all our Summer Birds it is at all events that of very many," he noted with delight as the south not only showed him new birds, but old friends from the north.

Southern Aviary

One of the first birds they noticed as they arrived in New Orleans was a fish crow. Gangs of fish crows were foraging around the docks for food. The streets teemed with a great variety of people. At New Orleans' main market, a wide array of freshly killed waterfowl and even songbirds were for sale. In the crowds, Audubon lost his wallet to a pickpocket.

After his time on the river, New Orleans seemed busy. Audubon used his connections with local gentry to earn money painting portraits, and before the end of the month had accumulated almost $300 to send to Lucy. He no longer had time nor easy access to hunting for new bird species to draw.

In March 1821, Audubon's father-in-law died. Then Audubon got word that a crew member of Aumack's flatboat had found Audubon's lost portfolio. Only one drawing was missing.

Mason did not enjoy the hustle and bustle of New Orleans, but with Audubon's encouragement, he focused on drawing the abundant plant life.

small portfolio of 15 drawings was missing. Most likely it had been left on the wharf. Three of the drawings were of birds that were new species to him. There had also been a portrait of Lucy. He worried that the drawings would be found by a boatman who had no idea of their value or importance, and they would be lost forever, like his drawings that had been destroyed years before by rats. "I am aboard a keelboat going down to New Orleans the poorest man on it," he wrote the following day.

Trying not to dwell on the loss, Audubon was soon immersed in observing the scenery and the bird life. The woods were teeming with warblers

For months Audubon had been trying to be selected as the artist on an expedition into the Red River country to the Gulf of Mexico, or another to Florida, but he soon gave up hope. He was offered a job teaching drawing and other subjects to the 16-year-old daughter of the owners of the large Oakley Plantation in hilly country upriver.

"The Rich Magnolia covered Odiferous Blossoms, the Tall Yellow Poplar, the Hilly ground, even the Red Clay I looked at with amazement . . . such entire Change in so Short a time, appears, often supernatural, and surrounded Once More by thousands of Warblers and Thrushes, I enjoyed Nature," he wrote. Then, to his delight, he sighted a Mississippi kite and a swallow-tailed kite, two birds he had long wished to see.

He and Mason were welcomed kindly and shown to their room at the plantation, with its separate entrance at the back of the house. It was as if he had been awarded a special retreat for drawing birds. He was being paid to teach in the mornings, all their meals were provided, and they had the

(left) **Fish crows are usually found near water.**

(right) **American redstarts.**

rest of the day and night to draw. Mason was now ready to draw the plants in each portrait of a new a bird that Audubon drew. Over the next three months they created about a quarter of the illustrations needed for his *Birds of America*.

One such illustration features the American redstart, a common warbler that winters in Louisiana. In it, Audubon captured the constant activity of the foraging male. "It keeps in perpetual motion, hunting along the branches sidewise, jumping to either side in search of insects and larvae, opening its beautiful tail at every movement which it makes, then closing it, and flirting it from side to side."

The drawings of the tree branch and wasp nest demonstrate Mason's skill, remarkable for a young

Black-billed cuckoos
in a magnolia tree.

teenager. Mason's talent is also evident in the magnolia in different stages of flowering in Audubon's depiction of black-billed cuckoos, a species that only passes through Louisiana on its journey to its wintering grounds in northern South America.

After three months of drawing and exploring an area rich with birdlife, Audubon witnessed his 16-year-old student, Eliza Pirrie, become seriously ill. During that time, Audubon produced work he knew was his best yet. He had plans to create even more, but Mrs. Pirrie dismissed him from his teaching job. He pleaded to be allowed to stay for another eight or ten days, so they could finish up their artwork and notes. He was not regretful about leaving the family with its imperious mother, alcoholic father, and coddled daughter, but he was reluctant to depart from the "sweet Woods."

A Reunion

Back in New Orleans, Audubon began searching for new students and soon found a small house with enough room for Lucy and the boys. In the year he had been away from them he had finished 62 drawings of birds and plants and over 50 portraits, which had supported him and Joseph, as well as Lucy and their sons.

A week before Christmas 1821, Lucy arrived with the boys and all of his earlier drawings. Looking through his past work, Audubon was elated to see how much better his new work was. Now he set himself the goal of supporting his family and Mason with income from teaching, while he continued to create new bird portraits from specimens brought to him by hired hunters.

Within a few months he understood that he was once more unable to support his family while continuing to add drawings of new species to his portfolio. He and Lucy were unhappy with their poverty. William Brand, a wealthy friend and fan of Audubon came to the rescue by offering Lucy a job tutoring his young, pregnant wife. Once again Lucy was supporting the family.

John James decided to go to Natchez with Mason to pursue opportunities to teach and make portraits. Through new friends in Natchez, he soon was employed drawing portraits and teaching at a school for young women outside of town. Now more secure with a steady job, he asked Lucy to join him. She sent the boys but said she felt obligated to stay with young Mrs. Brand until her baby was born.

Again John James had steady work but no time for his passion. Like many young, unestablished artists or actors, having to pay the bills diminished his chance for success. "I feared my hopes of becoming known to Europe as a naturalist were destined to be blasted," he wrote in his journal.

In late summer Mason, now 15, left for Cincinnati. His two-year apprenticeship with Audubon had prepared him for work as an artist. Audubon gave him his old shotgun and art supplies.

In September, Lucy joined her family in Natchez, and within a few months a friend of John James found her a job as a teacher on a plantation called Beechwood. It was not far from the Oakley Plantation and was home to a great variety of birds. John James painted once more and was fascinated by the large number and size of alligators.

He also continued to write about bird behavior. "Often the blue jay, Thrush, white-eyed flycatcher (vireo) and other small birds may be heard scolding some animal concealed in a thicket about which they flutter."

Birds have a neighborhood alert system for when a predator is on the prowl or merely present. A roosting owl discovered by songbirds will soon be surround by screeching, chipping, agitated birds who will dart back and forth, but not close enough to be snatched in its bill or talons. The loud racket produced by upset birds often provides bird-watchers with an opportunity to view a seldom seen predator, whether it be a weasel, snake, owl, or hawk. Nest-robbing species such as crows, jays, and ravens are often witnessed being taunted and chased by much smaller birds desperately trying to protect their eggs or nestlings. Other species hearing them will join in the attack because the predator is a danger to the entire bird community.

John James was hired to paint portraits of the daughters of Mrs. Percy, the mistress at Beechwood. She strongly objected to the slightly yellow tone of the girls' skin in his paintings. In the racially mixed society of Louisiana, skin color signaled children born of slaves and slaveholders. It is possible that the girls had a yellow pallor due to having malaria, a common ailment of that era. Audubon objected to her criticism, and she asked him to leave. Off he went with his son Victor to Natchez in search of work as a portrait painter.

False Alert

Bird-watchers who wish to get a better view of hidden birds sometimes try to get them to come out into the open by making imitation alarm calls. If the birders are lucky, curious birds will come out to see what the fuss is.

YOU WILL NEED:

↘ Binoculars

↘ Bird-Watching Journal

↘ Penn or pencil

Visit a bird-rich site where you rarely see other birdwatchers. Scan the plants in the area for birds, especially trees and shrubs. You may just glimpse the movement of birds in the foliage.

There are two kinds of alarm calls that are fairly easy to make:

Peeshing: With your lips together, push out some air to make your lips vibrate and sound like *peesh*. Do this as loudly as you can for a minute or two while looking around for any birds that emerge from foliage to see what is going on.

Kiss Chirp: Hold one hand up to your mouth and make a loud kissing sound with your lips. It should sound like a bird chirp. Scan for birds that have come out from hiding.

Were you able to flush out any birds? Did one call work better than the other? Record anything you learned or observed in your Bird-Watching Journal.

Warning: Making alarm notes disturbs birds, so be respectful and do it only occasionally. In places where many birders have used alarm calls, birds may not respond. Some bird-watchers will play a recording of a male bird's song from a smartphone or other device. This can be harmful because it can greatly disturb male birds that then neglect feeding or caring for their young.

Audubon worked all summer on a panoramic landscape painting for a wealthy widow for a generous fee, but his bad luck would return. The widow died before she paid his fee, and her heirs refused to honor her promise. Then in August both John James and Victor came down with yellow fever. John James's good friend Dr. Provan took them under his care and alerted Lucy. She immediately left Beechwood for Natchez to nurse them back to health.

In September Mrs. Percy wanted her skilled teacher back and said that all was forgiven, and John James could come live there once more.

Back North

Lucy had made arrangements with her sister Eliza and her husband to take on Victor as an apprentice clerk in Shippingport.

In October 1823, John James and Victor boarded a steamboat heading upriver. Partway up the Ohio River, the low water prevented the steamer from going any farther. With no horse available, John James decided to reach Louisville by foot, a distance of 250 miles (402 km). Victor had turned 14 in July, and both of them were newly recovered from yellow fever. They walked the distance in just over a week.

Though Lucy's sister and her husband Nicholas welcomed their nephew Victor, they showed little warmth toward John James, believing he was only chasing impossible dreams with his desire to publish his book *Birds of America* instead of supporting his family. There, in the neighborhood where his

business had been, he was reminded daily of his failure to succeed in it.

John James missed Lucy, and he had doubts about the success of his planned journey to find a publisher for his book. After arriving in Philadelphia in April 1824, he met Charles Lucien Bonaparte, nephew of French Emperor Napoleon Bonaparte, who had died three years before. Charles was a talented biologist with a special interest in birds and had been welcomed by the Academy of Natural Sciences.

Bonaparte was astounded by Audubon's art. Expecting to see more birds in stiff unnatural poses, he saw lifelike, life-size birds in natural settings and poses that showed how and where they lived. For the following weeks Bonaparte took John James with him around Philadelphia to introduce him to many of the city's prominent artists and scientists.

Many were impressed by him and his work, but others, like George Ord, an influential member of the academy and a close friend of Alexander Wilson, took an immediate dislike to Audubon. He called his art gaudy, thought that the inclusion of plants made the paintings too busy, and considered him a man without honor or reputation.

Audubon was rejected by the Academy. No one wanted to publish his work. Nonetheless, he did make friends and found artists who admired his skill. One engraver who praised Audubon's art urged him to seek publication in England where he thought he would find more opportunity. With his hopes temporarily deterred, John James returned to Lucy in Louisiana.

5

TAKING A LEAP

....

After a long ride journey back to Beechwood, Audubon finally arrived at the plantation. "It was early, but I found my beloved wife up and busily giving a lesson to one of her pupils. I held and kissed her. All toils and trials were forgotten. I was once more, happy."

Mrs. Percy allowed John James to stay in the cottage with Lucy and John Woodhouse until he completed his collection of paintings and saved enough money to leave for England. He started teaching French, music,

Peregrine falcons. Audubon called them great-footed hawks.

Dusky petrel, later known as Audubon's shearwater.

and drawing classes at Lucy's school and ballroom dancing in the barn. He was also asked to teach fencing to the three sons of a judge 15 miles (24 km) away in Woodville, Mississippi. Since it required a long trek two days per week, he also taught dancing there. The earnings from large group dancing lessons helped increase their savings.

No longer poor, John James and Lucy enjoyed being together, playing music, dancing, and swimming. Lucy also took notes on Audubon's new observations when he returned from outings. Audubon wrote to Charles Bonaparte to inform him of new observations. In one letter, he criticizes Alexander Wilson for claiming that wood ducks are never found in flocks. He stated that flocks of juvenile wood ducks were so large that they attracted many hunters.

John Woodhouse, or Johnny, now almost a teenager, joined John James on hunting excursions

and helped collect insects to send to scientists. They collected specimens together, and the collection of paintings grew. One of them dramatically portrayed blue jays in the act of stealing another bird's eggs.

England

After one and a half years with his wife and younger son, it was time for Audubon to leave for England to seek a publisher for his *Birds of America*. He departed the day before his 41st birthday and over 20 years since he had first started his project. He stored his precious cargo of 300 pictures in tin-lined portfolios. In his wallet he carried $1,700 (almost $40,000 in 2020). He also carried with him letters of introduction from DeWitt Clinton, senator and previously governor for New York, as well as from the governor of Louisiana and Henry Clay, an influential politician from Kentucky. This he hoped would open doors for him with important people in England.

He sailed off, bound for Liverpool, on May 18, 1826, aboard the *Delos*, soon after its cargo of 924 bales of cotton was loaded. Once they got out to sea, the going was slow due to a lack of wind. A month later, they were still near the western shores of Florida where Audubon was intrigued by the flight of a bird he called a dusky petrel. He observed that when the birds fly over the water in search of fish to hunt, after "flapping their wings 6 or 7 times in quick succession," they glide for an almost equal amount of time before flapping again. "Raising and falling with such beautiful

Field Trip to a Different Ecosystem

A trip to the seashore, the desert, a forest, or a marsh will give you opportunities to see birds that you might not see in your home community.

YOU WILL NEED:

🐦 Bird-Watching Journal

🐦 Pen or pencil

🐦 Binoculars (optional)

Depending on where you live, the seashore, the desert, or the mountains could be a completely different ecosystem than the one you're familiar with. At the seashore there will be birds along the edge of the water such as sandpipers; others in the air, like gulls and terns; and others floating in the sea itself, such as scoters, pelicans, and cormorants.

Record the birds you spot in you Bird-Watching Journal. As you observe these birds, consider how they are suited to conditions that do not exist where you live and how that determines their appearance and behavior.

When you return home, compare the species you identified in your home ecosystem with those you found in the new ecosystem. Were any the same? How many were in one ecosystem and not the other?

The black scoter is common on ocean waters.

ease to motions of the waves that one might suppose they receive special power to that effect from the Element below them."

Unknown to him at the time, this species would later bear a different name, one in his honor: the

Portrait as backwoodsman painted by John Syme, 1826.
WikiCommons

Audubon's shearwater. *Shearwater* refers to their habit of skimming closely over the water. While Audubon examined one, he noted its strong fishy smell. He sketched a life-size portrait of a specimen. Later in *Birds of America*, his picture offers a unique view that allows us to see its legs and feet through the water.

Once in the open seas, away from large numbers of birds, one day faded into the next. To occupy his time, Audubon sketched members of the crew and passengers. He read every book aboard, most twice, learned to plot longitude and latitude, and fished. After two months he was becoming bored and anxious to reach the shores of England. He also became anxious about his success at finding supporters for his book. Down in the sleeping quarters, mice and cockroaches roamed freely, and each day the aroma of unwashed bodies grew more potent.

The ship arrived in Liverpool on July 21, 1826, and Audubon with his long flowing hair strode onshore wearing his backwoods buckskin attire. He had decided to play the part of the American woodsman.

Now Audubon was in a new country, a whole ocean away from his family and beloved America. For most of his adult life he had followed his passion for learning about and depicting the birds of the United States. He was mostly self-taught in both writing and art.

To follow his dream, he had to be apart from Lucy and his sons for long periods. He had been judged as irresponsible by Lucy's family, as well as friends. During his 20 years of creating his artwork, John James had to constantly earn money by doing portraits or teaching. The result of his labor, his great accomplishment, was a portfolio weighing over 100 pounds and containing the hundreds of pictures that were his life's work. Would the hard-earned money that he and Lucy had saved for this venture be enough to support him while he pursued his task of getting *Birds of America* published?

Audubon desperately needed to find wealthy and notable people who would not only praise his art, but also subscribe to *Birds of America*. To produce this book that would be like no other, he had to locate a printer capable of reproducing his art.

The first thing Audubon did on his arrival was go to the business of his brother-in-law Alexander Gordon, who had married Lucy's sister Ann. Audubon hoped for a warm greeting but instead received an unfriendly welcome from Gordon, who had once been a friend. Gordon not only failed to invite him to his home to see Ann, but also said if he wanted to see him again he could come to the office. Like other members of Lucy's family, he blamed Audubon for his business failure in Henderson. Audubon was deeply hurt.

Success at Last

To sell his vision for *Birds of America* would take the confidence and charm of an experienced salesman. Fortunately for Audubon, his artwork would speak for itself. John James built up his courage and contacted Richard Rathbone, to whom he had a letter of introduction. The Rathbone family

William Roscoe, portrait by Martin Archer Shee. *WikiCommons*

were wealthy Quaker cotton merchants, abolitionists, and influential members in the artistic and cultural community of Liverpool.

Rathbone received him warmly and invited him to a gathering of the family at his mother's home. There, Audubon showed his artwork, and they enthusiastically commented they had never seen such fine art. Their honest praise buoyed his spirits.

The Rathbones shared their delight with other influential citizens of Liverpool, and within a week of his arrival, Audubon met with William Roscoe, a major figure in Liverpool society who opened doors for Audubon. On the last day of July,

Audubon had an exhibit of his portfolio at the Royal Institution of Liverpool. During the third day of the exhibit, 413 people jammed in the room to see his art. He was becoming the talk of the town.

Old town Edinburgh was noted for its narrow alleys. *WikiCommons*

Soon after this triumph, Audubon set off for the home of a business partner of the Rathbones who had arranged a meeting with Sir Edward Stanley, an aristocrat, noted ornithologist, and member of parliament. Audubon was so nervous he said his hair stood on end. Stanley greeted him with warmth and then got down on his hands and knees to examine Audubon's artwork.

After carefully examining the pictures for five hours, "He praised my drawings and I bowed to him," Audubon wrote in his journal.

Within a short time of his arrival in Liverpool, Audubon had received approval from the notable people he had wished to impress. The day after his triumphant meeting with Lord Stanley, he wrote, "Every object known to me smiles when I meet it, and my poor heart is at last relieved the great anxiety that has for so many years agitated it, by [the feeling that] I have not worked altogether in vain."

He dined that evening with the Rathbones, and after the meal entertained them by imitating the call of the wild turkey, the hoot of a barred owl, and the cooing of doves.

The earnings from his exhibit prompted Audubon to take his art on tour. Manchester, where he next showed his portfolio on September 21, did not attract the crowds or yield the same earnings as his show in Liverpool. But he did make some important contacts and was fortunate to meet with a successful bookseller who thought Audubon's artwork was superb and worthy of publication, but not in a large format. Later, that same bookseller, after viewing Audubon's exhibited artwork, agreed that it should be published in a large size, called double elephant—pages roughly 27 inches by 40 inches (69 cm by 102 cm)!

Audubon continued north to the Scottish city of Edinburgh, where he hoped for more positive reviews of his portfolio in addition to finding a publisher. By his third day there, he had met a printer who soon introduced him to William Lizars, a printer with experience reproducing images of birds. During the previous few years, he had printed the naturalist and artist Prideaux John Selby's large-size folio *Illustrations of British Ornithology*. The art was finely executed and accurate, but not nearly the superior quality of Audubon's work.

When Audubon showed the printer his artwork, Lizars exclaimed, "My god I never saw anything like this before!"

The following day, Lizars came to visit Audubon at his lodgings accompanied by Robert Jameson, a highly respected professor at the University of Edinburgh. Jameson "says he will, with my permission, announce my work to the world, and I doubt not I shall find him an excellent friend," Audubon wrote.

Later that day he had a visit from Patrick Symes, a flower painter who would soon paint Audubon's portrait.

On Lizars's next visit, Audubon showed his large drawings, the hen turkey, the hawk attacking a covey of quail, and the whooping crane tearing and devouring newborn alligators. "All were, he said, wonderful productions; . . . but when the Great-Footed Hawks came with bloody rags at their beaks' ends, and cruel delight in the glance of their daring eyes, he stopped mute an instant, then said, '*That* I will engrave and publish.'"

Later Lizars said, "Mr. Audubon, the people here don't know who you are at all, but depend upon it they *shall* know."

Flying High

Lizars's words about Audubon becoming known to people in Edinburgh came true when his work was exhibited at the Royal Institution of Edinburgh, Scotland's national academy of science and letters. The exhibit was a great success, earning the equivalent of $13,500 in 2020 money from admission fees. It also received glowing reviews, such as the following from a French critic: "A magic power transported us into the forests which for so many years this man of genius has trod. . . . On twigs, branches, bits of shore, copied by brush with the strictest fidelity, sport the feathered races of the New World, in the size of life. . . . This picture of nature so lusty and strong. Is due to the brush of a single man, such an unheard-of triumph of patience and genius!"

Audubon couldn't have been more pleased by this praise for his art. He was welcomed into Edinburgh society by scientists, artists, and aristocrats.

"I go to dine," he wrote, "at six, seven, or even eight o'clock in the evening, and it is often one or two when the party breaks up; then painting all day, with my correspondence, which increases daily, makes my head feel like an immense hornet's nest, and my body wearied beyond all calculation; yet it has to be done; those who have my best interests at heart tell me I must *not refuse* a single invitation."

Best of all, Lizars had started the work of reproducing five of Audubon's bird portraits, the first of which was a large tom turkey and the second, the yellow-billed cuckoo snagging a butterfly in a paw-paw tree. On the day he saw both prints he wrote in his journal, "My situation in Edinburgh borders on the miraculous."

He had found an excellent engraver and was celebrated for his life's work. Despite this, he was exhausted and homesick for Lucy and the boys. He missed his American forests, swamps, and bayous. He thought that the natural landscape in Great Britain was degraded after years of taming by humans. He could now foresee the same fate for the lush nature of his adopted home if something wasn't done to stop the deforestation, the rerouting of rivers, the leveling of hills, and the filling in of swamps. The grandeur would be gone. "Millions of songsters will be drove away by man," he wrote in his journal.

He was invited to the immense home and estate of the Earl and Lady Morton. He gave the Lady drawing lessons, and she subscribed to *Birds of America*. He was awed by the request of ornithologists Selby and Jardine to teach them his special techniques used to create his pictures. One of the most important tips he passed on was to place birds on the center of gravity.

At the beginning of January 1827, the first five plates of *Birds of America* had been printed, and by February 5, after being colored by hand, were dis-

played at the Royal Society of Edinburgh. Audubon's colleagues were so astounded by the power and quality of the prints that they unanimously elected Audubon a foreign member of the society.

Through the rest of the month, Audubon prepared for his trip to London, the most populated city in Europe. He collected letters of introduction to important residents of the city and finalized printing arrangements with Lizars. The hand-colored engravings would be on the finest double folio size paper. A set of 5 prints would be produced at a time, called a number, and there would be 5 of these printed each year. The projected 80 numbers would take at least 16 years to produce. The price for printing alone would be almost $50,000 ($1,300,000 in 2020). John James Audubon, who once went bankrupt, would have to find the funds to pay for all this.

His departure was delayed by harsh weather that included a blizzard on March 12 that dropped 16 feet (4.8 m) of snow! His sister-in-law Ann, the Rathbone women, and Lady Morton all encouraged Audubon to cut his long locks and buy clothes that would be more appropriate for an English gentleman. Though he was used to his long hair and comfortable in his unique backwoods garb, Audubon listened to them. When he finally did depart for London, he looked like a different man.

By April, Audubon was ready to start his journey of more than 400 miles (644 km) to London. He traveled to Newcastle upon Tyne, where he had an exhibit and met the legendary wood engraver Thomas Bewick. While gazing out the

Composition Center of Gravity

How a picture is composed determines how we view it. A visual composition that draws the viewer's eyes to the geometric center of the picture gives a feeling of balance. A composition with the main figure in a corner or along the edge gives a feeling of uncertainty. Is the figure going to fly off the page?

Look at Audubon's picture of the great-footed hawk (peregrine falcon) on page 56. Can you feel your eyes being drawn to the center where the two birds' bills are almost touching? The bright red blood on the bill of the righthand hawk further directs your eye to the center. These elements impressed Audubon's printer when he first viewed the piece.

Audubon's composition of the Carolina parakeet pulls the viewer's eyes to the bird in the center, while at the same time depicting a very active scene with parakeets feeding on cockleburs in a swirl of motion. Your eye takes in the action going from one yellow and orange head to another, so that you can almost hear the wild racket of the hungry birds.

· ·

YOU WILL NEED:

↘ Bird-Watching Journal

↘ Pen or pencil

↘ Colored markers or pencils

Sketch the outline of a bird or birds just below the center of a blank page in your Bird-Watching Journal. Consider how to pose the bird or birds so that the viewer's eye will go directly to them. For example, you may choose to draw a small flock of sparrows that you see on the ground, or jays in a tree or shrub. You can change their actual positions to make a composition that draws the viewer's eyes to the center. It may be easiest to redo one of your previous birds' portraits, but with center of gravity in mind.

Carolina parakeets.

The Real Poop

Birds digest food rapidly so they won't be weighed down by full stomachs. They also do not pee. Water is heavy, so carrying it around to eliminate excess salts and urea would make flight less possible. Instead, birds eliminate uric acid along with other wastes, such as invertebrate exoskeletons and seeds, through their droppings.

Birds usually excrete their droppings (poop) just before takeoff. Birds such as mockingbirds eat berries and dispose of the seeds in their droppings. The seeds' hard coats are worn down by the birds' stomach acids, which readies them to sprout when conditions are right. These seeds are encased in rich fertilizer, providing them with nutrients necessary to grow.

• •

YOU WILL NEED:

↘ Bird-Watching Journal

↘ Pen or pencil

↘ Magnifying lens (optional)

Watch your neighborhood birds closely when they take off into the air. Can you see their "poop" being ejected? **Warning**: Do not touch bird droppings or get your mouth or nose close to them. Over 60 diseases have been found in bird droppings!

Look for bird droppings on car windshields and beneath trees where birds roost or feed. You should be able to see both white and darker parts. The white is uric acid, and the dark is non-digested food. If you have a magnifying lens, study the contents and write about them in your Bird-Watching Journal.

Look underneath wires or branches where birds often perch. Can you discover any plants that sprouted from droppings? Ornamental shrubs with berries, such as pyracantha and privets, are spread by birds ejecting seeds in their droppings.

window of his lodging, Audubon watched bank swallows (called sand martins in England) flying by. He wrote, of them, "They seem indeed as if created for the purpose of spending their time on wing, for they alight less often to rest when full grown than any other of our species."

Audubon continued south, adding ten new subscriptions in York, another five in Leeds, and more in Manchester and Liverpool. With his new subscribers in city after city, he had more than doubled his total to 94.

London

After his arrival in London on May 21, 1827, Audubon found himself in an immense city, teeming with humanity. It was dirty, noisy, and mostly devoid of nature.

He made his way through the throng of people, trying to connect with prominent people to whom he had letters of introduction. Most were out when he visited. Fortunately, John George Children was at his office at the British Museum. Children was head of the museum's Department of Zoology and secretary of the Royal Society of London. He was impressed by Audubon and his art. That night, Children brought Audubon to a meeting of the Linnean Society, where his first set of prints enthralled many of those present.

In his journal, Audubon wrote that London was "like the Mouth of an immense monster, guarded by millions of sharp-edged teeth, from which if I escape unhurt it must be called a miracle. I have many times longed to see London, and now I am here I feel a desire beyond words to be in my beloved woods."

Audubon was questioning his decision to come to big, monstrous London, not realizing that it was the place he needed to be when he received news from Lizars that production of the finished prints had come to a halt. The workers who colored the engravings had gone on strike for higher wages. Lizars wondered if Audubon could locate some colorists in London who could do the work there.

Off he went, searching in the poorer part of the city for someone who could do the work. He witnessed poverty and slums worse than any he had seen before. Families were starving not far from the large, stately houses occupied by the extremely wealthy.

As luck would have it, Audubon was directed to the shop of a skilled London engraver and publisher, Robert Havell Sr., but it was two days before he found the printer in his shop. Audubon's art wowed Havell, who said he was not in the position to do the engraving but could oversee the printing and coloring. He promised to hire a competent engraver.

Audubon accepted his terms. An engraver/publisher friend of Havell's had showed him an engraving of a landscape that greatly impressed him. "That's the one for me," said Havell, and to his shock the friend said, "Well then send for your own son." After a vicious argument in the past, Robert Havell Sr. and his son Robert Havell Jr. had not seen each other for years.

Strangely, Audubon had initiated a reconciliation between a father and son in order to bring *Birds of America* into being. The senior Havell had chosen a talented engraver to work for Audubon, without knowing it was his own son. This was fortunate for both father and son, who were now ready to forgive past behaviors. It was also fortunate for Audubon, who now had two skilled printers ready to reproduce his work. Not only would the Havells' work cost less than Lizars's, but their work was of much better quality. Robert Havell Jr. used a technique called aquatint that produces tones from gray to black, enabling him to reproduce the shading and shadows in Audubon's original art.

By November, Audubon was profiting from his subscriptions. Equally important, he was feeling strong enough not only to keep pace beside a walking horse but also to outwalk a horse on a 20-day trip, by his own estimation. Best of all, he got news from John George Children that King George IV had subscribed.

Unlike other bird books, which placed each species in the taxonomic order determined by Swedish scientist Carl Linnaeus, the order in *Birds of America* was determined by the visual impact the lineup of birds would have on the viewer. *Birds of America* was meant to be a work of art carefully based on the appearance, habits, and habitat of each species. It was to be a visual tour of the birds he had come to know and love during his life.

Like most artists, Audubon examined his art with a critical eye. He became more skilled the more he worked on his art. As he looked at earlier work, he saw the difference between pieces he had done years ago and the one he had more recently completed, and he saw the need to redo or revise ones like his portrait of a bald eagle.

"This morning I took one of my drawings from my portfolio and began to copy it, and intend to finish it in better style. It is the White-headed Eagle, which I drew on the Mississippi some years ago, feeding on a Wild Goose; now I shall make it breakfast on a Catfish, the drawing of which is also with me, with the marks of the talons of another Eagle, which I disturbed on the banks of that same river, driving him from his prey. I worked from seven this morning till dark."

It had been almost two years since he had parted from his family. He missed America and "longed to look at a blue sky" instead of London's yellowish, coal-tainted atmosphere. At the beginning of May, a review of his first printed images appeared in a popular natural history magazine. Its author, a British naturalist by the name of William Swainson, claimed Audubon's art portrayed the passions and feelings of birds. He praised his genius and passion and stated there were no other artists that were his equal.

Swainson and Audubon became friends. Audubon visited the Swainson family 20 miles (32 km) northwest in Tyttenhanger Green, where he enjoyed conversations about birds and walks in the countryside.

Despite these diversions, producing *Birds of America* was taking up the majority of his time. To pay for the cost of printing, he also had to create paintings to sell to add to the money from subscriptions. He had to visit the Havells' print shop one or more times a day to oversee the quality of the prints. During the summer of 1828 he worked on no fewer than eight paintings at a time, from dawn until dark.

Audubon later named the Swainson's warbler after his friend.

Paris

On September 1, Audubon, William and Mary Swainson, and a visiting landscape painter from Natchez left for Paris. After arriving there, all except Mary went to the Jardin des Plantes to meet with Georges Cuvier, a giant in the world of science, though he stood less than five and a half feet (1.7 m) tall. When Audubon informed Cuvier that he had named a wren after him, he earned his interest. Later, under Cuvier's sponsorship, Audubon sat in the seat of honor at the Academie Royale des Sciences and presented his portfolio, which earned praise and admiration of the members.

Audubon was welcomed by Baron Francois Gerard, a renowned French painter, who told him after viewing the mockingbird and paroquet plates, "Mr. Audubon, you are the king of ornithological painters. . . . Who would have expected such things from the woods of America!" And in a report to the Academie Royale des Sciences in September, Cuvier wrote that *Birds of America* was "the most magnificent monument which has been erected to ornithology."

Audubon was disappointed by the small number of subscribers he had obtained after more than a month in France but also realized that this country was not as wealthy as England. Of the 14 he got, one was from Charles X, King of France.

Audubon had achieved a remarkable feat, gaining praise for his bird portraits from French and British scientists and artists. Now he had another massive goal to achieve, the production of a book like none had done before. It would take a great amount of money, as well as oversight of the printing to ensure it was done correctly. Audubon looked forward to sending the completed sets of plates to subscribers.

Now, at the start of 1829, he realized that he had to paint pictures of the species he had yet to illustrate and improve the quality of some that were yet to be printed. He would have to return home. He was no longer a free man. *Birds of America* was now his chief, and he had to do what was necessary to complete it.

It was almost three years since he had been with Lucy and their sons. Being apart from them had been painful for him, but he would have to wait a little longer. He would not be able to go to them right away when he arrived in America because it would be prime season for finding the species he still needed to illustrate. He would have to devote himself to his art for long hours each day. John George Children of the British Museum offered to help with the subscriptions and take care of his art while Audubon was away.

By now Audubon had complete trust in his printer Robert Havell Jr., whom he would supply with the art, 25 original pieces. He would be away for the next 12 months.

On April 1, 1829, Audubon boarded the packet ship *Columbia* bound for New York. Along with him he brought a hunting dog, a spaniel that was a parting gift from the Rathbones.

6

THE BUSY BACKWOODS ARTIST

. . . .

After his arrival in New York on May 5, 1829, Audubon immediately exhibited a bound volume of 50 prints at the New York Lyceum, where he had been made a member five years earlier.

He then traveled to Camden, New Jersey, in time to observe and draw great numbers of warblers on their way north. One that he drew was the

Osprey. Audubon also called it the fish hawk.

71

blackpoll warbler, a bird he knew and wondered about, but had never drawn.

"[The blackpoll warbler] enters Louisiana as early as the middle of February. At this time it is seen gleaning food among the taller branches of the willows, maples, and other trees that overhang the rivers and lakes. Its migrations eastward follow the advance of the season, and I have not been able to comprehend why it is never seen in the maritime parts of South Carolina, while it is abundantly found in the State of New Jersey close to the sea-shore."

He also knew that they nested in the far north and wondered why he had never seen them south of Cape Hatteras on the North Carolina coast.

The mystery of their migration wasn't revealed until the spring of 2015, when data from miniature tracking devices attached to migrating blackpoll warblers showed that they flew directly from the East Coast of North America to northern South America, a three-day nonstop flight across the Atlantic Ocean. Some flew from Vermont and Nova Scotia, Canada, to western Long Island or New Jersey for a stopover before flying south to Puerto Rico or the Island Hispaniola, a distance of more than 1,600 miles (2,574 km), all of it over open water with no rest. After stopping, they continued across the Caribbean Sea to Venezuela or Columbia to spend the winter.

The energy for such a journey takes stored-up fat that is accumulated as the bird gorges on insects prior to flying south. A blackpoll's average body weight is 0.4 ounces (12 g) (the weight of an empty soda can). Before departing on their southward migration, these birds generally gain another 0.3 ounces (8 g) that are stored in fat deposits.

After three weeks near Camden, Audubon headed to Great Egg Harbor on the New Jersey coast. "There I had the good fortune to be received

Blackpoll warblers.

into the house of a thoroughbred fisherman-gunner, who, besides owning a comfortable cot only a few hundred yards from the shore, had an excellent woman for a wife, and a little daughter as playful as a kitten, though as wild as a Sea-Gull. In less than half an hour I was quite at home, and the rest of the day was spent in devotion."

Egg Harbor, named by the Dutch for its abundance of seabird eggs, offered a great variety of land and sea birds. Audubon called one the grass finch, now known as the vesper sparrow.

"It sings sweetly, and at times for half an hour, without changing its place. . . . During this little serenade it is easily approached, but when on the ground, where it runs nimbly and with grace, it is rather shy. It is fond of scratching in the warm and dry sand, and of wallowing in it, to cleanse its body. Its flight, which is easy, consists of a succession of gentle undulations, and, when it is chased, sometimes extends over the whole of a field."

Seeing and listening to birds from his seaside cot, feasting on fresh oysters and just caught fish was the life he had so missed during his time in England. He completed 20 new drawings. One of these was his iconic eye-level depiction of an osprey. Later he wrote, "Fish Hawks are very plentiful on the coast of New Jersey, near Great Egg Harbour, where I have seen upwards of fifty of their nests in the course of a day's walk."

He still missed Lucy and their sons and was anxious to see them. His life was now devoted to doing everything he could to complete *Birds of America*.

Vesper sparrow next to a prickly pear cactus, once common on the Atlantic seashore.

Into the Woods

When Audubon returned to Philadelphia, he met up with George Lehman, a Swiss born landscape painter whom he had met five years before. This was a stroke of good fortune for Audubon, who needed backgrounds for his new paintings. Lehman agreed to paint backgrounds for a month.

Now Audubon was ready to return to the woods, this time the Great Pine Swamp about 40

The blackburnian warbler feeds on small insects and spiders in the upper canopy.

miles (64 km) northeast of Philadelphia. There he hoped to find more birds that he needed to draw. He arrived at the home of Jediah Irish in the heart of the forest during a drenching thunderstorm. The next day, guided by Irish's nephew, he found and procured a species that had evaded him for years. This small bird, with its orange-yellow colored throat and yellow head stripe, lives in the upper level of a forest, called the canopy. From the ground it is not easy to see. Alexander Wilson collected one and described it in his book, *American Ornithology*. Claiming it was a new species, he named it the hemlock warbler because of its preference for hemlock forests, though it is also found in spruces, firs, and pines.

Unknown to Wilson, his "new" species was a female blackburnian warbler. The blackburnian warbler had been scientifically named in 1776 by a German zoologist. Audubon was elated to finally be able to draw Wilson's "hemlock warbler," not knowing that it had been previously named.

By mid-August, Audubon had collected and drawn four more species of warblers. Another bird he had seen in many locales, from Louisiana to Massachusetts, was the pileated woodpecker. Here in the Great Pine Swamp, he watched them foraging on tree trunks. He noticed how they struck the bark sideways on the harder barked hemlocks and spruces, while they chiseled away the bark of softer barked trees in a straightforward manner.

Audubon now needed their portrait for his book. In the picture, one of the woodpeckers holds a large beetle grub in its bill. Two young males are shown facing each other, their lighter colored bills distinctly longer than those of the adults. Audubon wanted to show this difference in bill size. He later wrote in his account of this woodpecker how the bills on the juvenile birds were flexible at the tip, and the young birds avoided hammering trees. Instead, they foraged for insects in very rotten wood and ate berries, as well as a favorite treat, carpenter ants.

Audubon's ten weeks in the Great Pine Swamp restored for him inner peace and outer strength. It was also a productive time during which he added 30 more drawings of bird species to his portfolio.

Changing World

Audubon was now 44 years old, and since the beginning of his explorations 20 years earlier, he had seen great changes to his beloved woods. The forest of the Great Pine Swamp, which he stated was a forest, but not a swamp, was disappearing right before his eyes. "Trees one after another were, and are yet, constantly heard falling, during the days; and in calm nights, the greedy mills told the sad tale, that in a century the noble forests around should exist no more. Many mills were erected. . . . One full third of the trees have already been culled, turned into boards, and floated as far as Philadelphia."

Audubon's days in the more heavily populated England, where vast forests had been turned into open grassland, had given him a look into America's future. Gone were the once abundant wild turkeys, and numbers of grouse were only "tolerably abundant."

From June through early autumn, Audubon worked on collecting birds and drawing them. He woke early, relying on as little as four hours of sleep each night. By October 10, he felt he had added enough "missing" bird species to his portfolio. More importantly, he had been able to

Pileated woodpeckers.

immerse himself once again in his "woods." He decided to rejoin his family.

"I am at work and have done much, but I wish I had eight pairs of hands, and another body to shoot the specimens; still I am delighted at what I have accumulated 62 drawings this season.

"I returned yesterday from Mauch Chunk; after all, there is nothing perfect but *primitiveness*, and my efforts at copying nature, like all other things attempted by us poor mortals, fall far short of the originals. Few better than myself can appreciate this with more despondency than I do."

Audubon was very socially adept. He had spent the last few years in England befriending wealthy, educated aristocrats, but he was also able to bond with what were considered common folk. As he left the forest for Philadelphia, he reflected on his time roughing it with the much younger Jediah Irish. He felt proud that at the age of 44 he was still able to enjoy the simple life of days outdoors, exploring and dining on wild game cooked over an open fire. He believed "closet" naturalists, who worked inside studying specimens collected by other people, would be better off spending days in the wood with people like Irish.

Back in Philadelphia, Audubon was delighted that George Lehman had completed the background art for 42 drawings. One was of the grass finch (vesper sparrow) of Great Egg Harbor, in front of the once common eastern prickly pear cactus, New Jersey's only native cactus.

By the end of the month, Lehman completed more, including one of the "hemlock warbler" placed in a dwarf maple, a small tree that grows in the forest understory. Audubon shipped all the new drawings, plus drawings of the eggs of 60 bird species, to his printer Robert Havell.

Reunited

Now that Audubon had completed his tasks, he could visit his family. His first stop would be to visit his sons, Victor Gifford and John Woodhouse.

From Philadelphia, he rode a coach to Pittsburgh. The road had improved since he and Lucy had traveled it many years before, but it wasn't good enough for Audubon. He wrote, "The slowness of the stages is yet a great bore to a man in a hurry." Staying only a half day in Pittsburgh, John James boarded a ship to Louisville. When he entered the counting house of his brother-in-law William Bakewell, he barely recognized his son Victor, who had a job there. In the five years since they had parted, Victor had grown into a tall, handsome young man.

Audubon had changed too. No longer dressed in rough woodsman's clothing, he now appeared a fine gentleman in his classy London apparel. Father and son embraced and then together walked the two miles (3.2 km) to Shippingport, where John Woodhouse worked at his brother-in-law Nicholas Berthoud's business.

At last, he was with his beloved sons, but his darling Lucy waited in Louisiana. Two days later, he left on a steamboat for Bayou Sara. Since his last time on the river, much had changed. He wrote in his journal, "When I see that no longer any Aborigines are to be found there, and that the vast herds of elks, deer and buffaloes which once pastured on these hills and in these valleys, making for themselves great roads to the several salt-springs, have ceased to exist; when I reflect that all this grand portion of our Union, instead of being in a state of nature, is now more or less covered with villages, farms, and towns, where the din of hammers and machinery is constantly heard."

Audubon lived during a time of enormous change. Between 1807, when he had first settled in Louisville, and 1829, when again he was traveling down the river, the population of the United States had almost doubled.

During the last few years that he was parted from Lucy, he worried that their marriage may have changed for the worse. He arrived in the middle of the night on November 17 in Bayou Sara. Beech Grove Plantation, where Lucy had her school, was still 15 miles (24 km) away.

He needed to find a horse. He knew that yellow fever was ravaging the area, and when he entered a familiar inn, he could sense death. He finally reached the house of a friend who lent him a horse, and he took off, joyfully riding through the dark woods that he loved.

John James reached the plantation after dawn and rushed to Lucy's apartment, where he found her awake and teaching piano to a young woman. He called softly to her and soon "I held her in my arms. Her emotion was so great I feared I had acted rashly, but tears relieved our hearts, once more we were together."

While Lucy waited another month to collect school fees owed her, John James spent the time drawing, painting, and collecting species of birds and plants. He found what he thought was a new species of hawk that he named *Harlani*, after his Philadelphia friend Richard Harlan, and gave it the common name, black warrior. He drew both the male and female alive after both had been winged (wounded in the wing by shot). The pair had been roosting near the plantation.

Harlan's hawks, a subspecies of red-tailed hawks. Audubon called them black warriors.

BIRD DISTRIBUTION

Our knowledge of where birds breed, migrate, and spend their winters does not come from one single ornithologist roaming the Earth. Bird-watchers around the world keep track of what they see and share that knowledge with other bird-watchers. In Audubon's day, communication between scientists around the world was slow due to a dependence on mail, which moved at a snail's pace. Today, there are internet sites such as eBird that help scientists communicate discoveries instantly.

Audubon realized the birds were similar to a red-tailed hawk, even though they lacked the distinctive rusty colored tail. For many years, Harlan's hawk was considered a distinct species; later it was determined to be a subspecies of the red-tailed hawk. The bird winters in Louisiana, Texas, Kansas, and Nebraska, after breeding in the taiga, conifer forests of the Yukon Territory and Alaska in the far northwest.

Lucy and John James Audubon left Bayou Sara on New Year's Day 1830, accompanied by her three slaves, Celia and her two sons, Reuben and Lewis, who Lucy had by her side for nearly 20 years. One of the many cruelties of slavery was that slaves could be sold at will. Celia and her sons would soon be sold to the Audubons' friends, the Brands.

John James paid for two staterooms on a steamer heading upriver. Once, while the boat was stalled due to engine trouble, Audubon went ashore and collected twenty Carolina parakeets, two ivory-billed woodpeckers, and two pileated woodpeckers for their skins. Two of these once abundant species, the Carolina parakeet and the ivory-billed woodpecker, would no longer exist 100 years later. The rapid destruction of forests, and over hunting, erased them from the American landscape.

After arriving in Louisville, the Audubon family was reunited. Although John James Audubon was finally together with his family, it would not last nearly long enough. He had to return to England to deal with decreasing subscriber numbers. At least Lucy would now be with him. Audubon explained in detail all that must be done to complete *Birds of America*, and how he needed his family to help him. He promised that as soon as he raised more funds through more subscriptions, he would have the money to send for Victor and Johnny.

In early March, Lucy and John James left for Cincinnati to visit Lucy's brother Thomas and then traveled to West Virginia to see her sister Sarah. They then continued to Washington, DC, to meet with President Andrew Jackson, who greeted them warmly. John James Audubon—a chambermaid's illegitimate son, a derided businessman in Henderson, and an American backwoodsman famous in England—was now recognized as an important citizen by the president of the United States!

They next met with Massachusetts representative Edward Everett, an influential leader in Congress and a former publisher. Everett was impressed by Audubon's work. He arranged for an exhibit at the House of Representatives and convinced Congress to purchase a subscription.

Before departing for England on April 1, Audubon obtained three more subscriptions in Baltimore.

On April 2, 1830, he and Lucy boarded a packet ship in New York bound for Liverpool. Lucy had not been in the country of her birth for close to 30 years and looked forward to seeing her sister Ann. They arrived April 27, the day after John James's birthday. The American woodsman was now 45 and was back in England with his "best friend."

7

NEW WORK, NEW HONORS, AND PROBLEMS

....

Lucy found her sister Ann very ill when they arrived at her home in Liverpool. It was most likely from an infection caused by giving birth. Fortunately for Ann, Lucy cared for her with devotion for the next three months, during which her condition worsened before finally getting better.

Swainson's hawk.

Meanwhile, John James went to Manchester to exhibit his new illustrations and to assure disgruntled subscribers who were upset by the poor coloring of the recent prints that new correctly colored plates would be sent to replace them. Audubon communicated to Robert Havell the need to closely supervise the work of the colorists and added that there were no problems with the engraving.

Visit eBird

Before you look for birds you haven't yet seen in your neighborhood, you can check where the bird has been seen on eBird, a site sponsored by the Cornell Lab of Ornithology.

• •

With an adult's permission, go to eBird.org to register and record your sightings. You can post your observations on the site, too. You'll find lists of birds seen in every state, and maybe even in your county or town.

If you have an upcoming trip to visit family or friends in another town or state, check out eBird for their town before you go. Bring binoculars, a bird field guide, and your Bird-Watching Journal with you, in case you have time to look for birds while you are there.

Once in London, Audubon received the astounding news that he had been elected a Fellow of the Royal Society of London. Now he stood among giants of science of the previous two centuries, from physicist Sir Isaac Newton to astronomer James Bradley and botanist Sir Joseph Banks. The only other American so honored was Benjamin Franklin, for his discoveries in electricity.

Despite Audubon's ability to promote himself and his work to fellow naturalists, he did not see himself as a scholar. When he expressed these doubts to his friend Charles Bonaparte, Bonaparte praised Audubon for his focus on thorough observation and fieldwork. Bonaparte wrote, "It is the facts, the observation made with judgement & especially with confidence which increase the scope of science."

Once sister Ann had recovered, Lucy was able to join John James on his travels, checking on subscribers and seeking new ones. Off they went to Birmingham, Manchester, Leeds, York, Scarborough, and Newcastle on their way to Edinburgh.

A New Project

The couple arrived in Edinburgh in mid-October and took lodging with John James's past landlady. Here, Audubon planned to start writing his companion volumes for *Birds of America*, which he titled the *Ornithological Biography*. Despite his many years speaking, reading, and writing in English, Audubon rightly decided he would need a collaborator who would edit this work. A friend referred him to naturalist and university lecturer William

MacGillivray, who was not only interested in the job, but also could start immediately.

Settled in with Lucy in Edinburgh, John James got started on his new project with his typical discipline and energy. "Writing now is the order of the day. I sat at it as soon as I woke in the morning and continued the whole long day, and so full was my mind of birds and their habits that in my sleep I continuously dreamed of birds. I found Mr. MacGillivray was equally industrious."

As Audubon wrote about each species, he remembered his past experiences observing them, as well as what he had learned about each species from other ornithologists. The process of writing immersed him in his past 25 years of exploration. Reminiscing about the locations of his encounters with individual birds, whether it be the Ohio River Valley or Bayou Sara, helped him describe each bird species in a personal narrative.

His first entry in Volume 1 of the *Ornithological Biography* is about the wild turkey. In it he writes about a specific incident he observed while on the banks of the Wabash River in Indiana: "While once sitting in the woods, on the banks of the Wabash, I observed two large Turkey-cocks on a log, by the river, pluming and picking themselves. I watched their movements for awhile, when of a sudden one of them flew across the river, while I perceived the other struggling under the grasp of a Lynx."

Watching an animal caught by a predator is something he was bound to remember, and if not, he surely would have recorded the event his journal. His plan was to write detailed accounts about the birds pictured in his first 100 plates. He also

Building a Bird Nest

Intricate nests like that of the marsh wren are constructed solely with the use of the bird's bill and feet. Now it's your turn to build a nest.

• •

YOU WILL NEED:

↘ Nest-building materials: grasses, fiber from dry plant stems, horsehair (if available), spidersilk, and other natural material

↘ Mud (optional)

↘ Camera or smartphone (optional)

↘ Bird-Watching Journal

↘ Pen or pencil

Like making a basket, start by tying flexible plant stems into the shape of a cross, and then build off that. You can also start by coiling soft stems to create a base that you can build up from. Continue to weave grass, twigs, and other material to make a secure nest. (Some birds, such as phoebes or swallows, add mud to glue it together.) As you build the nest, think about the size of the bird that would use it and if there will be enough room for eggs and the parent bird perched on top. When it is complete, look for a well-hidden place on a tree, shrub, or the ground to place it.

Take a photo or sketch the nest once it is in place. Write any notes or questions you have about building the nest in your Bird-Watching Journal.

Marsh wren
and nest.

wrote 20 "episodes," stories describing American life in a variety of locations, from his adventure in the Great Pine Swamp to his experience with the New Madrid Earthquake. In his tale titled "The Prairie," he tells a suspenseful story about nearly being murdered by the bloodthirsty thieving sons of an old woman while staying at her cabin. He tells readers that this was the only time during 25 years of exploring that he felt his life threatened by other people.

The final bird described in Volume 1 is the marsh wren. Audubon provides a description of the nest pictured in his illustration: "The nest is nearly of the size and shape of a cocoa-nut, and is formed of dried grasses, entwined in a circular manner, so as to include in its mass several of the stems and leaves of the sedges or other plants, among which it is placed. A small aperture, just large enough to admit the birds, is left, generally on the south-west side of the nest."

Day by day during the short days of Scottish winter, John James added more pages. He later wrote, "and so the manuscript went on increasing in bulk, like the rising of a stream after abundant rains, and before three months had passed the first volume was finished."

In four months, John James completed his writing, and MacGillivray had edited the 582-page Volume 1. Meanwhile, Lucy copied the entire manuscript to send to Dr. Richard Harlan in Philadelphia, who was helping to get it copyrighted. Lucy also joined John James in the many publishing and bookkeeping tasks required to complete both the biography and the printing of plates.

By April 1831, Volume 1 of the biography was in print in England and received an enthusiastic review from a respected magazine. Everything was going well. Being back with Lucy and having his printer producing pages at top speed meant that John James could return to the United States. Havell would soon need new drawings to print from, and John James had to once again explore for new bird species to illustrate.

Just days before their departure on July 31, Audubon met with his wealthy young friend Edward Harris, who had helped him years before when he was desperate for money after an unsuccessful exhibit in Philadelphia. Harris had not only purchased all his unsold pictures, but also handed him $100, saying, "Mr. Audubon, accept this from me; men like you ought not to want for money." In his honor many years later, John James gave the name Harris's hawk to a species new to science.

Lucy and John James sailed from Portsmouth accompanied by a young taxidermist, Henry Ward, hired to assist in making bird skins. They arrived in New York on September 4, 1831.

New Territory, New Friends, New Birds

Lucy's sister Eliza now lived in New York City with her husband Nicholas Berthoud, who had moved his business there. After a week's visit, they joined Victor in Philadelphia, who traveled from Louisville to join them. He would accompany his mother back to her brother William's home in Louisville while John James went off to Florida.

Audubon hired George Lehman, who had painted backgrounds for his paintings from Great Egg Harbor and the Great Pine Swamp, to do the same on their planned journey to Florida. Together, Lucy, Victor, John James, and Henry Ward traveled to Baltimore. While there, John James and Victor met with the Secretaries of Navy and Treasury, who gave permission for Audubon, Lehman, and Ward to use US revenue cutters—armed ships employed by the government—for transport on their expedition.

Congressman Edward Everett, future governor of Massachusetts and future president of Harvard University, arranged for an exhibit of Audubon's newest prints at the Library of Congress. He had also nominated Audubon as a member of the American Academy of Arts and Letters and was working to allow Audubon's publications enter the United States duty-free.

After an emotional farewell to Victor and Lucy, Audubon headed south with his cohorts. Victor and Lucy continued on to Louisville. Despite the excitement of another journey of discovery, Audubon once more was sad to be parted from his family.

On their journey south, Audubon wrote about his delight in being in "country bounded as is always in America by woods, woods, woods!"

Since the goal of the journey was to follow autumn migrants to Florida, they continued on their way, arriving on the bank of the Cooper River. They crossed it by canoe and landed in

Charleston, South Carolina, where good fortune awaited them. They first found a boardinghouse where they could stay, but it was too expensive. Audubon had a letter of introduction, among the many he carried, for Reverend Gilman, who took him on a walk to find cheaper lodging. As they strolled, a man on horseback, Reverend John Bachman, greeted his fellow minister, who introduced Audubon. On hearing the name Audubon, he quickly dismounted and with a large, friendly grin shook Audubon's hand. He had heard of Audubon and, being a naturalist himself, dearly wished to host a man he so admired. He urged Audubon, Lehman, and Ward to stay in his spacious house. They accepted his offer and, as John James wrote Lucy, they moved there in "a crack!"

Long-billed curlews.

Bachman and his wife Harriet, her sister Maria, nine children (seven of them girls), and their two grandmothers were living in the large home. Surrounding the three-story house were gardens and trees, an aviary in the back, duck pens, and slave quarters.

Audubon and Bachman had much to discuss about birds and *Birds of America*. Bachman joined him as he returned to his wood-hunting habits, rising before dawn to collect, take views, or draw birds in the last light of day. In Charleston's marshes they collected great blue herons, yellow-crowned night herons, cranes, and common egrets, keeping Ward busy preparing skins. Ward skinned 220 specimens of 60 different species by the end of the first week in November. Audubon had learned that he needed skins of new species to verify his discoveries and skins of all species he painted to later compare with his final art.

Audubon too, was busy, having completed nine drawings during his first two weeks in Charleston. During that time, he also managed to meet many important citizens of the city, including a medical doctor who gave him Plato, a beautiful black and white Newfoundland retrieving dog.

On November 7, Audubon and his friends traveled to Cole Island about 20 miles (32 km) away to collect more water birds. Chief among these was the long-billed curlew, an odd-looking bird with a long down-curved bill four times the width of the head that it uses for probing in sand and mud for crabs and sea worms.

In the morning, the curlews flew off from their nightly roost to search for food, and they returned at the end of the day. "As the twilight became darker the number of Curlews increased, and the flocks approached in quicker succession, until they appeared to form a continuous procession, moving not in lines, one after another, but in an extended mass . . . directly towards their place of rest, called the Bird Banks."

In his portrait of them, Audubon shows a male curlew about to probe for food and the female with her head up, appearing alert as if she were looking at the viewer. These curlews, despite their fishy flavor, were sold in markets for 25 cents each ($7.50 in 2021). Hunting reduced the numbers of long-billed curlews enough that by the end of the 1800s, their very existence was threatened.

Florida

Being in Charleston with the Bachman family and his many new friends was a pleasant experience, but Audubon was on a mission to find new species to illustrate for his book. It was time to head south to new territory with unique birds.

Before he left, Audubon wired up an American bittern skin for Bachman's sister-in-law, Maria Martin, to draw. Martin would later draw plants, her specialty for Audubon's paintings.

On November 15, 1831, Audubon, Lehman, Ward, and the hunting dog Plato boarded a packet ship bound for Florida.

St. Augustine was disappointing to Audubon. What had once been the Spanish Empire's capital of East and West Florida was now a backwater. Oranges and fish were the city's source of income.

After an hour of hard rowing, he and Lehman would be in the middle of vast marshes. Then they waded through mud and water and were attacked by clouds of mosquitoes and sand flies. The heat made it necessary for them to draw the birds soon after killing them because the feathers would lose their colors, and the flesh would quickly spoil.

Just before leaving St. Augustine, Audubon shot a "hawk of great size, entirely new." He quickly sketched the specimen from above and below, which later was used to compose his drawing of two of the birds grappling in air. It wasn't until later that Audubon found out that it was a crested caracara, a member of the falcon family. This was one bird that Alexander Wilson did not encounter, but an Englishman had described 10 years before Audubon's birth. The crested caracara in Florida is isolated from other populations in Texas, Mexico, and South America. It is known today as Audubon's crested caracara and is struggling to survive in Florida due to loss of habitat.

On January 15, a war schooner, the *Spark*, arrived, and Audubon showed the captain his letters from the Secretaries of Navy and Treasury guaranteeing passage on the ship to pursue his mission of collecting birds. The captain agreed that Audubon and his helpers could come along on a cruise up the St. Johns River while the captain and crew surveyed oaks for use in future shipbuilding.

First the *Spark* had to sail up the Atlantic coast for 40 miles (64 km) to reach the mouth of the river and then follow the river south. When they were about 100 miles (161 km) upriver, one of the sailors

Crested caracaras.

afternoon, and they waited for the wagon, which never appeared. Together they decided that Audubon, Lehman, and Plato would walk to the coast while Ward stayed with the gear. As they departed, a storm was approaching, and night was descending.

"Plato was now our guide, the white spots on his coat being the only objects that we could discern amid the darkness, and as if aware of his utility in this respect, he kept a short way before us on the trail. . . . Large drops began to fall from the murky mass overhead; thick impenetrable darkness surrounded us, and to my dismay, the dog refused to proceed. Groping with my hands on the ground, I discovered that several trails branched out at the spot where he lay down; and when I had selected one, he went on. Vivid flashes of lightning streamed across the heavens, the wind increased to a gale, and the rain poured down upon us like a torrent."

Soaked to the bone, they tramped for hours through brush and partly flooded prairie. Just as they became worried that they were lost, they smelled the aroma of salt marshes. Soon they saw a beacon near the city. Before long, they reached their hotel and dispatched a wagon to pick up Ward and their gear.

Rather than wait in unproductive St. Augustine for another navy vessel, they booked passage back to Charleston on the same ship that had brought them south.

Back in Charleston, Audubon got to work collecting new specimens and drawing. During his five weeks there, he completed five new pictures.

accidently shot himself, and the captain decided to return to St. Augustine to get the sailor medical care.

Audubon wanted to return to St. Augustine faster and arranged for two local men to take him, Lehman, Ward, Plato, and their gear downriver to a place where they would be met by a wagon. Once they reached the drop-off point, it was late

One was of a sparrow that John Bachman had collected in a pine forest. Audubon later wrote, "Since then I have heard as many as five or six in the course of a morning's ride, but found it almost impossible to get even a sight of the bird. This was owing, not to its being particularly wild, but to the habits it possesses of darting from the tall pine-trees, where it usually sits to warble out its melodious notes, and concealing itself in the tall broom-grass which is almost invariably found in those places which it frequents."

This was another bird that Wilson had missed. Audubon named it Bachman's finch in honor of his friend. Today it is known as Bachman's sparrow.

Another bird Audubon painted during this time was the snowy egret. These birds would feed in the thousands in rice fields and saltwater marshes. Maria Martin, Bachman's sister-in-law, painted a watercolor copy of his drawing while he offered advice on the composition. When a naval vessel, the US revenue cutter *Marion*, came into port, Audubon arranged passage for him and his companions. He left his new drawings with Martin to embellish.

They departed in mid-April. Audubon was delighted that the pilot, named Egan, knew birds. "The pilot, besides being a first-rate shot, possessed a most intimate acquaintance with the country. . . . Not a Cormorant or Pelican, a Flamingo, an Ibis, or Heron had ever in his days formed its nest without his having marked the spot; and as to the Keys to which the Doves are wont to resort, he was better acquainted with them than many fops are with the contents of their pockets."

With help from Egan, Audubon encountered dozens of pelicans, hundreds of cormorant nests, egrets, herons, gulls, and terns. At Cape Sable at the southern tip of the Florida peninsula, Audubon saw the odd-looking roseate spoonbills. He explains their feeding behavior:

To procure their food, the Spoonbills first generally alight near the water, into which they then wade up to the tibia, and immerse their bills in the water or soft mud, sometimes with the head and even the whole neck beneath the surface. They frequently withdraw these parts however, and look around to ascertain if danger is near. They move their partially opened mandibles laterally to and fro with a considerable

Roseate spoonbill.

degree of elegance, munching the fry, insects, or small shell-fish, which they secure, before swallowing them.

On Sandy Island, six miles (9.6 km) from Florida's southern tip, Audubon was overwhelmed by the sight of birds covering the beach. "Rose-colored Curlews (curlew sandpipers) stalked gracefully beneath the mangroves, purple herons (Louisiana herons) rose at almost every step we took, and each cactus supported the nest of a White ibis. The air was darkened by whistling wings," wrote Audubon.

This was the Florida he had been hoping to experience. At Indian Key, a third of the way down the chain of keys (coral islands) at the southern tip of Florida, a local showed Audubon a heron he had never seen before. It was the size of a great blue heron but completely white! He drew it with the label *great white heron*. Now it is considered to be a color variant of the great blue heron.

BIRD BILLS

Bird bills (beaks) vary greatly among the many species. Birds like the roseate spoonbill are named for the shape of their bills, while others bear names that reflect the size of their bills: evening grosbeak (large bill), long-billed curlew, and short-billed dowitcher. Other names, like black-billed cuckoo, red-billed tropicbird, and yellow-billed magpie, refer to the color of their beaks. Weebill beaks are the size of a pencil tip, while those of Australian pelicans reach a length of one and a half feet (0.5 m).

On his 47th birthday, Audubon drew a Florida cormorant (a double-crested cormorant subspecies), which he had taken down with one shot, where thousands of birds were nesting in the mangroves near the key. During the days that followed, he collected and drew roseate terns, brown pelicans, and white-crowned pigeons, species found in South Florida, the Keys, and the islands of the Caribbean.

Finally, in early May Audubon and his companions arrived at Key West, a free-spirited community of 500 souls at the extreme southeastern point of the United States. Most residents made a living from scavenging ships that wrecked on the nearby reefs. He contacted Benjamin Strobel, a physician friend of John Bachman's, who advised Audubon on the best locations to find birds. Strobel wrote in the local newspaper about his excursion with Audubon: "At three o'clock [AM] we started. . . . Our boats were hauled over a flat nearly a mile in length before we could get them afloat. . . . Not a pond, lake, or bog did we leave unexplored, often did we wade through mud up to our knees, and as often were obliged to scramble over the roots of mangrove trees." He wrote about the heat, the clouds of mosquitoes, and sand flies. Despite their hardships, they had not discovered a bird worthy of note. By mid-morning, the doctor called it quits, while the rest of the group continued on. "Mr. Audubon is the most enthusiastic and indefatigable man I ever knew."

Audubon pursued birds needed for his book day after day. During the second week in May, he traveled west on the *Marion* to the Tortugas, small islands where sooty tern and noddy tern (now called brown noddy) nested.

The Noddies form regular nests of twigs and dry grass, which they place on the bushes or low trees, but never on the ground. On visiting their island on the 11th of May, 1832, I was surprised to see that many of them were repairing and augmenting nests that had remained through the winter, while others were employed in constructing new ones, and some were already sitting on their eggs. In a great many instances, the repaired nests formed masses nearly two feet in height, and yet all of them had only a slight hollow for the eggs, broken shells of which were found among the entire ones, as if they had been purposely placed there.

Brown boobies nest on islands in the tropical waters of both the Atlantic and Pacific Oceans.

North of the Tortugas, they encountered a colony of booby gannets (brown boobies) nesting on a sandbar barely above sea level. Wondering about their name (*booby* means "stupid"), he wrote, "I am unable to find a good reason for those who have chosen to call these birds boobies. Authors, it is true, generally represent them as extremely stupid; but to me the word is utterly inapplicable to any bird with which I am acquainted."

On another of the islands, Audubon encountered egg harvesters from Cuba. "They had already laid in a cargo of eight tons of both (sooty) and the noddy eggs," Audubon later wrote. So many eggs were taken that finally the colony

Brown booby.

needed protection as a special conservation area to prevent the noddies from disappearing as they had from several nesting colonies on small keys in Jamaica.

When Audubon later traveled along the far northeast coast of the United States and into Labrador, he once again witnessed massive harvests

BIRDBRAINS

Calling someone a birdbrain implies that the person has inferior mental abilities. But birds are highly intelligent creatures. How many people can remember where they placed their car keys, let alone thousands of sites where they buried seeds months ago, some of which are covered by a meter of snow? The Clark's nutcracker, a bird of western North America, may collect up to 98,000 whitebark pine seeds in mid-summer and bury them in caches of 1–15 seeds (3–4 on average) over hundreds of acres. The seeds will be their food in February and March when they nest. They bury more than they need and recover a large percentage of their hoard. The seeds not recovered may sprout, thus ensuring that a new generation of pines is added to old-growth forests. Clark's nutcrackers, like their near relatives—crows, ravens, jays, and magpies—raid songbird nests for eggs and young. Nutcrackers are known to wait a few weeks after discovering a new songbird nest before they return to eat the nestlings, showing that they time their raid to get a bigger meal—nestlings instead of eggs.

of seabird eggs, which resulted in the elimination of seabird nesting colonies on islands of New England. This had to do not with the stupidity of birds, but with humans who had no knowledge or concern that their actions would cause the end of their livelihood.

Back North

On the return trip north from Key West, Audubon traveled on a barge from Indian Key to Cape Sable, the western tip of the Florida peninsula, to search for waterbirds missing from his drawings. He was frustrated by not being able to get close enough to observe them with his naked eyes. When onboard a seagoing vessel such as the *Marion*, he would borrow a spyglass from the crew.

Observing birds, particularly waterbirds, was a challenge without the binoculars and scopes available today. Audubon wrote, "The Land Bird flits from bush to bush, runs before you, and seldom extends its flight beyond the range of your vision. It is very different with the Water Bird, which sweeps afar over the wide ocean, hovers above the surges, or betakes itself for refuge to the inaccessible rocks on the shore."

The *Charleston Courier* reported Audubon's return to Charleston in early June. He stayed there with the Bachman family for almost a whole month, until he departed for Philadelphia via coach. He left behind his dog Plato and young Henry Ward, who now had a job at the Charleston Museum as a taxidermist. Rather than stay in Philadelphia to wait for Lucy and their sons to arrive, he left for Camden, New Jersey, where lodging was cheaper. While there, he collected and drew more bird portraits, including a ghostly pair of barn owls.

By the middle of July, Lucy, John Woodhouse, and Victor had reached Philadelphia, which they left in a hurry to avoid a dangerous outbreak of cholera. It had reached North America from Europe for the first time. They arrived in New York City to visit Lucy's sister Eliza and her husband Nicholas, who now lived there. People were also fleeing New York City to escape this dreaded disease. Of those who stayed, 3,000 of them perished.

Now the Audubon family, which had not been all together for 13 years, were heading north to Boston and beyond. John James needed both of his sons to help him with his great project. Victor would assist with the business side of *Birds of America*. Johnny, who was more of a happy-go-lucky young man, but physically active and artistic like his father, would help with collecting and preparing skins of new specimens and with drawing new bird pictures.

Audubon was touched by the warm reception he received in Boston. An exhibition of his drawings appeared at the Boston Athenaeum, a revered old library. He added nine more names to his list of subscribers. He had the pleasure of going into the field with Thomas Nuttall, the legendary botanist and zoologist known for his explorations in America's Northwest and the headwaters of the Missouri River. Nuttall taught at Harvard University.

During their walk, Audubon collected an olive-sided flycatcher, a species first described by Nuttall.

A Boston Winter

With the arrival of summer, the Audubon family headed north with the birds, traveling by boat and stagecoach and on foot to the coast of Maine and then Canada. During this journey, John James and his sons took treks into the fields and forests in search of birds.

In Dennysville, a small town in the far northeastern corner of the United States, they were welcomed by Judge Lincoln and his family. His son

Tom Lincoln joined Audubon and sons on excursions into the woods and led them to the quiet habitats of spruce grouse. People he met, who knew about birds, urged him to explore Labrador in Canada's extreme northeast.

Now was not the time though. That far north, summer was short and had passed. It was time to head south. Along the way, Audubon found some birds that he still needed to picture. Finally, they arrived back in Boston.

Victor departed on October 16 on a packet ship bound for Liverpool, while Lucy, Johnny, and John James settled into a boardinghouse for the long, cold, Boston winter. Audubon set to work drawing and writing Volume 2 of *Ornithological Biography*,

Spruce grouse are found in forests around the northern part of the world.

which Lucy edited and copied to send to MacGillivray in Edinburgh to further edit. John James also gave art lessons to Johnny.

In February Audubon was given a golden eagle that had been caught in a fox trap. After studying it while still alive, he knew he must kill it if he wanted to draw it, though he was also tempted to let it free. He wanted the eagle to feel as little pain as possible. Thinking death from breathing carbonic gas would be most suitable, he tried that method, but it did not succeed. In the end, he had to pierce its heart with a long, thin piece of steel. The next step was to position the eagle, using mounting wires, with its wings beating as it lifts off into the sky.

Art historian Theodore Stebbins Jr. proposed that the composition of Audubon's golden eagle painting is based on a famous painting by Jacques-Louis David, *Napoleon Crossing the St. Bernard Pass.*

Audubon may have seen a colored engraving of the painting, or one of three versions David had painted—one was at Joseph Bonaparte's country

(left) *Napoleon Crossing the St. Bernard Pass* by Jacques-Louis David. *WikiCommons*

(right) **Golden eagle, original painting.**

estate in Point Breeze, New Jersey. The leftward facing eagle in Audubon's mountain scene echoes David's composition of Napoleon reared up on his horse. Also, a small figure appears in the bottom left of each composition. In Audubon's, it appears to be a self-portrait of the artist dressed in buckskin, and in David's painting, it is a foot soldier.

Audubon worked on his painting for 12 hours a day for five consecutive days. It is thought that he was perhaps trying to prove that, though his subject was birds, not people, he was an equal to David in his painting skills. When Richard Havell printed the portrait of the golden eagle, he eliminated the "self-portrait of Audubon straddling a log across the abyss."

It seems the intense effort he put into this work severely exhausted him. Shortly afterward, Audubon had a stroke, leaving his drawing hand temporarily paralyzed and Lucy terrified. In a month, he would be 48. He had depended on his vitality his whole life to accomplish great feats in exploring and composing art.

Within four days John James was recovered enough to write a letter to John Bachman. His planned expedition to Labrador had been delayed to give him time to recover, receive funds from Victor, and travel with Lucy to her sister's home in New York City, where she would stay while he and Johnny were gone.

Into the Cold North

On May 1, 1833, Audubon and son John sailed off from New York, reaching Eastport, Maine, the most northern coastal town in the United States, a week later.

The pair met up with the four young men who would assist them on the expedition. George Shattuck was a young Boston physician, and William Ingalls was a medical student also from Boston. Audubon dubbed them the "young gentlemen." Tom Lincoln had helped them hunt for birds in Dennysville, Maine, and Joseph Coolidge was the

Golden eagle print in *Birds of America.*

son of an Eastport revenue cutter captain. With Johnny as their leader, they would be responsible for the vigorous work of collecting specimens. John James would spend most of his time onboard their chartered schooner, the *Ripley*, painting pictures.

Before their final departure for Labrador, they went for a test run to Grand Manan Island 10 miles (16 km) northeast of Eastport at the opening to the Bay of Fundy.

Audubon wrote to Lucy:

The hold of the vessel has been floored, and our great table solidly fixed in a tolerably good light under the main hatch; it is my intention to draw whenever possible, and that will be many hours, for the daylight is with us nearly all the time in those latitudes, and the fishermen say you can do with little sleep, the air is so pure. I have been working hard at the birds from the Grand Menan, as well as John, who is overcoming his habit of sleeping late, as I call him every morning at four, and we have famous long days.

Indeed, the summer days were long so far up north. On a side excursion to Grand Manan Island to collect nesting seabirds, Audubon felt like he at last had recovered from his stroke and wrote, "I am Audubon again" in a letter to his friend Richard Harlan. For Audubon, his stronger-than-average physical ability was a key aspect of his identity, but he was now 48 years old surrounded by young energetic men, and he felt his age.

He wrote Lucy:

We are well provided as to clothes, and strange figures indeed do we cut in our dresses, I promise you: fishermen's boots, the soles of which are all nailed to enable us to keep our footing on the sea-weeds, trousers of fearnought so coarse that our legs look like bears' legs, oiled jackets and over-trousers for rainy weather, and round, white, wool hats with a piece of oil cloth dangling on our shoulders to prevent the rain from running down our necks. A coarse bag is strapped on the back to carry provisions on inland journeys, with our guns and hunting-knives; you can form an idea of us from this.

After departing on June 6, they all suffered sea-sickness crossing "the worst of all dreadful bays," the Bay of Fundy. A week after departing, they had reached the Magdalene Islands in the Gulf of St. Lawrence. Waking on June 13 aboard the *Ripley*, they shivered around the breakfast table where the thermometer measured 44 degrees Fahrenheit. They landed ashore on one of the eight larger islands where the temperature was milder.

Striding through the forest over blossoming strawberry plants, they listened to numerous songbirds. Along the beaches they spied piping plovers. Audubon commented, "These birds certainly are the swiftest of foot of any water-birds which I know, of their size."

Arctic terns were diving into the sea to catch fish. Audubon was entranced. He wrote later about the emotional struggle he went through when shooting birds to have in hand for drawing. He wrote:

Until that moment this Tern had not been familiar to me, and as I admired its easy and graceful motions, I felt agitated with a desire to possess it. Our guns were accordingly charged with mustard-seed shot, and one after another you might have seen the gentle birds come whirling down upon the waters. But previous to this I had marked their mode of flight, their manner of procuring their prey, and their notes, that I might be able to finish the picture from life. Alas, poor things! how well do I remember the pain it gave me, to be thus obliged to pass and execute sentence upon them. At that very moment I thought of those long-past times, when individuals of my own species were similarly treated [probably a reference to the executions he witnessed as a child in Nantes during the Reign of Terror]; but I excused myself with the plea of necessity, as I recharged my double gun.

This graceful species has the longest migration of any animal, traveling from the Arctic to the Antarctic and back each year, a journey, for some populations, of 57,000 miles (91,000 km). They breed across the arctic regions and winter (actually a second summer) in seas off the coast of Antarctica. During their lives, they experience more daylight than any other animal.

The following day, on their way north, the expedition spied what appeared to be a small rock on the horizon that increased in size the closer they got. It appeared to be covered in snow, but the pilot of the ship who had been there before said that the white color was from numerous birds.

Audubon wrote in his journal:

I rubbed my eyes, took my spy-glass, and in an instant the strangest picture stood before me. They were birds we saw, a mass of birds of such a size as I never before cast my eyes on. The whole of my party stood astounded and amazed, and all came to the conclusion that such a sight was of itself sufficient to invite any one to come across the Gulf to view it at this season. The nearer we approached, the greater our surprise at the enormous number of these birds, all calmly seated on their eggs or newly hatched brood, their heads all turned to windward, and towards us. The air above for a hundred yards, and for some distance around the whole rock, was filled with Gannets on the wing, which from our position made it appear as if a heavy fall of snow was directly above us.

The pilot, two of the sailors, Tom Lincoln, and Johnny set off from the ship in a whaleboat hoping to land on the rock, but it proved impossible with the rough seas and heavy rain. They managed to shoot a few gannets and retrieved the specimens for drawing and making bird skins. At close range, another aspect of the colony became overwhelming.

"The stench from the rock is insufferable, as it is covered with the remains of putrid fish, rotten eggs, and dead birds, old and young," Audubon recalled. "No man who has not seen what we have this day can form the least idea of the impression the sight made on our minds."

On their dives, northern gannets plunge many feet below the surface.

that they did not have an exterior nostril and that "Under the roof of the mouth and attached to the upper mandible, are two fleshy appendages like two small wattles," but it seems he did not know that these hard flaps ("wattles") covered thin slits along their jawline during a gannet's high-speed dives, which sometimes exceeded 50 mph (80 kph). When the bird was not diving, the slits remained uncovered to allow air to reach the nostrils inside the bird's mouth.

One day the group ventured ashore where there were brown mounds that appeared to be large rocks but turned out to be masses of moss. Walking across the moss was difficult, as they sunk knee-deep into the moss at each step. As they looked around, they could not see any spot with bare earth—there were no trees. Audubon, who felt so at home in forests, described it as a poor and miserable country. It was a completely different ecosystem from any he had yet visited, one that was harsh for human habitation.

The next day the sea was even rougher and the temperature colder as the rain continued. Everyone except Coolidge was seasick and cold. The weather improved by morning and remained good as they made headway northward to Labrador. The air was now filled with birds. Wild geese, eider ducks, loons, common murres, and razorbills were present in large numbers. Puffins, also known as sea parrots, "were in immense numbers, flying in long files a few yards above the water, with rather undulating motions," recorded Audubon.

Audubon spent days on board drawing, sometimes for up to 17 hours, until he could barely hold a pen or brush. One of the birds he drew was a gannet from Bird Rock, the northern gannet. With a wingspan greater than 6 feet (1.8 m), it is the largest seabird in the North Atlantic. The birds are found from northeastern coastal Canada to the other side of the Atlantic Ocean in Ireland, Wales, Scotland, and Iceland. Audubon noticed

Species in Danger

Audubon was amazed by the large numbers of birds and was happy to be learning more about the nesting habits, diet, and flight behavior of species totally new to him. He was also considering the attitudes and actions of his fellow humans:

The Wild Goose is an excellent diver, and when with its young uses many beautiful stratagems to save its brood, and elude the hunter. They will dive and lead their young under the surface of

the water, and always in a contrary direction to the one expected; thus if you row a boat after one it will dive under it, and now and then remain under it several minutes, when the hunter with outstretched neck, is looking, all in vain, in the distance for the stupid Goose! Every time I read or hear of a stupid animal in a wild state, I cannot help wishing that the stupid animal who speaks thus, was half as wise as the brute he despises so that he might be able to thank his Maker for what knowledge he may possess.

He was distressed by the massive plunder of seabird eggs to sell in cities and the killing of seabirds for codfish bait. He wrote, "We ascertained to-day that a party of four men from Halifax took last spring nearly forty thousand eggs, which they sold at Halifax and other towns at twenty-five cents per dozen, making over $800; In less than half a century these wonderful nurseries will be entirely destroyed, unless some kind government will interfere to stop the shameful destruction."

By 1909, 76 years after Audubon's visit to Labrador, ornithologists found seabird colonies greatly diminished in size. Some species, such as gannets and common murres (which Audubon called foolish guillemots), which previously existed in large colonies, were not seen at all.

Though distressed by this rampant destruction, Audubon felt at peace with the presence of songbirds that he had known throughout his years in America. One evening on a long northern summer day, he listened to an American robin singing. "The *Turdus migratorius* must be the hardiest of the whole genus. I hear it at this moment, eight o'clock at night, singing most joyously its 'Good-night!' and 'All's well!' to the equally hardy Labradorians."

On July 27, John James went ashore with Johnny and Tom Lincoln at the small settlement of American Harbor. They spied a bank swallow and heard blackpoll warblers singing. Audubon later described their song as one that "resembles the clicking of small pebbles together five or six times, and is renewed every few minutes."

They then heard a new song that startled them. Audubon wrote that the "sweet notes of this bird as they came thrilling on the sense surpassing in vigour those of any American Finch with which I am acquainted." The song seemed to burst forth, like a rushing stream, a flood of music that left the listener almost gasping. After the birds became aware of being watched, they dropped into the thick vegetation only to pop up on a branch farther away to renew their singing.

"We found more wildness in this species than in any other inhabiting the same country, and it was with difficulty that we at last procured it. Chance placed my young companion, Thomas Lincoln, in a situation where he saw it alight within shot, and with his usual unerring aim, he cut short its career." Audubon named this species new to science Lincoln's finch in honor of Tom. Today it is known as Lincoln's sparrow.

Returning Without Regret

Once again, the weather became cold, windy, and wet, making it appealing to go ashore, and difficult to draw with the ship rocking wildly. On July 30 Audubon wrote, "It was a beautiful morning when I arose, and such a thing as a beautiful morning in this mournful country almost amounts to a phenomenon."

Audubon and the young men went ashore for exercise, but the wind was so strong that they were happy to return to the shelter of the ship's cabin. The following days brought more wind, rain, and hordes of mosquitos. On August 10 Audubon described in his journal a gale so strong that the ship's anchor was dragged more than 100 feet (30.4 m).

Audubon and his team were tired of cold, windy, stormy weather. Audubon, who had endured mosquito-filled swamps and freezing winter storms, was not one to shy away from difficult conditions. But the climate of Labrador had bested him, and he was ready for the milder climes.

On August 11, the *Ripley* headed South toward Maine. "Seldom in my life have I left a country with as little regret as I do this," he wrote. Audubon was worn out by the harsh unsummerlike weather and sights of destruction by eggers, fisherman, and seal hunters. He was feeling old and uncomfortable with the challenging cold, windy conditions of Labrador.

By August 22, they were back in Pictou, Nova Scotia. Audubon and his young companions bid farewell to the captain and crew of the *Ripley,* whom they had become close to.

Audubon rejoiced at being in a place where the summer was summer:

We were now, thanks to God, positively on the mainland of our native country, and after four days' confinement in our berths, and sick of sea-sickness, the sea and all its appurtenances, we felt so refreshed that the thought of walking nine miles seemed like nothing more than dancing a quadrille. The air felt deliciously warm, the country, compared with those we have so lately left, appeared perfectly beautiful, and the smell of the new-mown grass was the sweetest that ever existed. Even the music of the crickets was delightful to mine ears, for no such insect does either Labrador or Newfoundland afford. The voice of a Blue Jay was melody to me, and the sight of a Humming-bird quite filled my heart with delight.

They traveled south by coach to Hailfax. Five days later they were amazed at the extreme tidal rise of 65 feet (19.8 m) in the Bay of Fundy.

They arrived back in Eastport, Maine, on the last day of August. To Audubon's delight, his friend Edward Harris was there to meet him with letters from Lucy and news of the wider world. It had been a challenging and expensive journey, costing nearly $2,000 ($57,000 in 2021), but Audubon felt it was well worth it. He now had 100 species unknown to both Wilson and Bonaparte.

A week later, he and Johnny arrived in New York, where they were welcomed with loving arms by Lucy at her sister's home.

Song Describer

Experienced ornithologists like Audubon were well aware of bird calls and songs, and any unfamiliar vocalizations immediately came to their attention. The more Audubon listened and learned about familiar birds, the more he developed an ability to describe them. To Audubon the robin sang a "goodnight song," the blackpoll warbler sounded like clicking stones, and the cooing of the zenaida dove was a soft and melancholy cry. Birders use varied language to describe bird voices. They sometimes compare them to musical instruments—the hermit thrush song is flutelike, and the Bullock's oriole song is described as trumpeting.

Audubon constantly listened to bird vocalizations. If he heard something that wasn't one of the everyday songs or calls he normally heard, he would pay more attention and scribble notes to help him remember it.

YOU WILL NEED:

↘ Bird-Watching Journal

↘ Pen or pencil

↘ Binoculars

↘ Field guide to birds

No matter where you live, during the warmer times of the year you will hear birds. Perhaps you recognize the squawk of a jay or the caw of a crow or raven. Bird-watchers have many words to describe bird sounds:

Verbs: Whistle, screech, chip, cheep, quack, honk, shriek, buzz, trill, boom, cluck, grate, grunt, croak, hiss, rasp, chatter, pipe, twitter, mew, bugle, bark, hoot, toot, squeal, gurgle, tinkle.

Adjectives: Explosive, soft, faint, nasal, clear, ringing, raucous, chatty, musical, mechanical, rough, smooth, liquid, sweet, sharp, clear, dry, insect-like, muffled, low, loud, wheezy, bubbling, clacking.

In this activity you can choose words from the lists on the left or come up with your own words to describe bird sounds that you hear. Some birds sound like they are calling a name. The tufted titmouse says *Peter, Peter, Peter*, while an acorn woodpecker sounds like it's saying *Jacob, Jacob, Jacob*. Write about what you hear in your Bird-Watching Journal.

If you are feeling creative, make up a word that sounds like a sound the bird is making, such as *spink, tseet, sree, chuk, krdee, chup, pew, teer,* or *pluk*.

If you can see the bird that is vocalizing, try to identify it using your field guide. Record its name next to your notes on its sounds.

8

BACK TO BACHMAN, AND THEN ENGLAND

• • • • • • • • • • •

What lay ahead for Audubon was more drawing and writing. Audubon preferred to be outdoors in wild places observing birds, but he had his massive *Birds of America* to finish as well as Volume 2 of his *Ornithological Biography*. By now he had proved himself a master artist and a proficient writer.

White ibis adult (white) and juvenile (brown).

Barn owls.

daughter Maria had fallen in love. Lucy and John James arrived on October 24.

John Bachman and his wife Harriet, their family of six daughters, two young sons, and sister-in-law Maria, welcomed them joyously. The three-story, 15-room house was spacious and comfortable for family and guests.

One day, Audubon was alerted to the presence of an owl nest in the upper story of an abandoned sugar house and was taken there by his friends who had seen it. Soon after the men entered the room, the parent bird flew out a broken window, leaving its chicks. Audubon later wrote in Volume 2 of *Ornithological Biography,* "The young were three in number, and covered with down of a rich cream colour. They raised themselves on their legs, appeared to swell, and emitted a constant hissing sound, somewhat resembling that of a large snake when angry. They continued thus without altering their position, during the whole of our stay, which lasted about twenty minutes."

Barn owls are the most widely distributed owl species on the planet and are found on all continents except Antarctica; they are only missing from north and western Asia. And yet, Audubon noted in his book, "none of the numerous European authors with whom I am acquainted, have said a single word respecting the time of breeding of this species."

Audubon was not only seeking out birds new to science but also looking for details about birds' habits that no other scientists had yet observed. To this day our knowledge of birds continues to grow and become more refined.

The Audubons planned to stay with John Bachman and his family in Charleston. Johnny left for Charleston ahead of his parents, for he was anxious to be with his beloved Maria. On a previous visit to the Bachman family with his father and brother Victor, Johnny and John Bachman's

Through winter, John James labored on entries for Volume 2 of *Ornithological Biography,* and Lucy transcribed his journal entries and notes to make the book writing easier for her husband. Johnny began drawing birds, and John James commented, in a letter to his son Victor, dated December 21, that John's compositions were "as good as any I ever made." He also told him he had nearly 100 drawings of water birds ready for publication and I pronounce them equal to any previous ones."

As in the goshawk painting, on some occasions Audubon cut out a bird from an older drawing and added it to a new composition. The immature goshawk in its natural active pose is an example of his mature artwork. The two other hawks are stiff, from older compositions that he added to the new one. As would be expected after so many years drawing, he was not only getting faster, but also improving the quality of his drawings.

At the start of December, Victor, who was overseeing the production of the printing in London, wrote to his parents, urging them to come join him in his challenging tasks. Since John James had arrived in Charleston, he had waited for news from the government that it could offer him use of a ship traveling south to Florida and west to the Gulf Coast as far as Texas. Thomas Nuttall and John Kirk Townsend were about to join Nathaniel Jarvis Wyeth's second expedition to the Pacific Northwest of America, where they would encounter a vast number of birds new to science. Audubon desperately wished he could join them to draw and add these "unknown" species to *Birds of America*. But he hadn't been invited and didn't have the time, due to his need to return to London to help Victor manage his publishing projects.

Back to the Monster

Audubon was no fan of London. He was not excited to return, but his life's work, *Birds of America*, depended on his shepherding it stage by stage until it was complete.

Purple grackles.

On April 16, 1834, Lucy, John Woodhouse, and John James Audubon boarded a 650-ton packet ship in New York bound for Liverpool, England. Though they traveled in comfort in the ship's best stateroom, Lucy struggled with seasickness and was relieved to reach shore on May 5.

After catching up with the Rathbones and other old Liverpool friends, they continued southward to London. John Woodhouse was awed by the size of London, and the family was overjoyed to be together once more. Victor had rented rooms near Cavendish Square, less than a mile from the British Museum and close to the large open spaces of Hyde, Green, and Regents Parks, and just a 30-minute walk to the River Thames.

Lucy and John James were proud of their sons' loving, loyal, and competent natures. Both were now studying music and art under the eyes of their father. And how pleased John James was that despite his absence for a good part of their childhood, they were following in his footsteps. Victor was painting landscapes, and Johnny was making black chalk portraits. Maybe because Victor had always been the more focused and responsible of his two sons, Audubon took for granted his many excellent skills, but was happily surprised by Johnny's work.

As soon as Audubon arrived back in London, he wrote to William MacGillivray, his friend and editor of *Ornithological Biography*, that he wanted him to continue to help with the project. MacGillivray responded that he was eager to proceed and that John James should send 25 "biographies" at a time.

Audubon's writing tended to be flowery and wordy. MacGillivray had the skill to trim each biography to make it both more concise and easier to understand. One of the species included in Volume 2 of *Ornithological Biography* was what Audubon called the yellow-crowned warbler, later known as Audubon's warbler. It was aptly named because, like Audubon, it is active, adaptable, and showy.

Audubon wrote, "The rows of trees about the plantations are full of them, and, from the topmost to the lowest branches, they are seen gliding upwards, downwards, and in every direction, in full career after their prey, and seldom missing their aim. At this time of the year, they emit, at every movement, a single *tweet*, so very different from that of any other Warbler, that one

A view of Cavendish Square showing a patch of green amid the growing city. *WikiCommons*

can instantly recognize the species by it among a dozen"

It was a long, hot summer. Audubon wrote more bird biographies and corresponded with friends, requesting information and bird specimens he so needed. As in the past, Audubon relied on his energy to write long hours, but he was now 49 years old. His hands swelled from overwork and slowed progress in drawing and writing. He wrote to Bachman saying he wished to return to the United States in the fall of 1835 to travel west, but he still had so much to get done in Europe first.

Early in September, Audubon headed north to try to drum up more subscribers, and just like in the past, he had to deal with rejection and impolite behavior with humility. He ended the trip in Edinburgh by meeting with MacGillivray and decided that going over the bird biographies would take months rather than a week or two. He wrote to Lucy asking her to join him there. Settled in Edinburgh for autumn, he wrote, and she copied. Audubon, like other adventurers who ended up writing, suffered from extreme frustration. In a letter to John Bachman, he wrote, "for my part I would rather go without a shirt . . . through the whole of the Florida swamps in musquito time than labour as I have hitherto done with the pen."

By mid-December, Volume 2 of *Ornithological Biography* was complete, and copies were sent to magazine editors. One review stated, "He [Audubon] has told what he has seen and undergone, not perhaps in the smooth nicely balanced periods of a drawing-room writer . . . but with unstudied freedom, rising at times to eloquence, nor been ashamed to utter the thousand affectionate and benevolent feelings which a close and enthusiastic communion with nature must nourish. The work is full of the man."

Meanwhile, John Woodhouse was busy painting portraits and completed 30 in October, including one of the Mayor of Edinburgh. There was cause for celebration when Volume 3 of *Ornithological Biography* was completed.

Return to the States

Bachman sent news that many plantations had been burned in the ongoing Seminole War in Florida. The US Army was unprepared for the fierceness of the Seminoles.

Early in 1836, the third volume of *Birds of America* was bound, and the first set of pages for the fourth and final volume had been engraved, one of them, plate 301, being of canvasback ducks with Baltimore in the background. Audubon wrote that a vast number of these ducks can be found in Chesapeake Bay and its tributary waters.

Lucy had been ill off and on throughout the year. John James was worried about her, but like in the past, she encouraged him to go. John James and son Johnny sailed for New York on August 2, 1836.

They arrived in New York City on September 7 planning to head south to Charleston, but a letter from Bachman warned them that cholera was plaguing that city and urged them not to come until it was safe. This delay greatly annoyed John Woodhouse, who was anxious to be with his beloved Maria.

Canvasback ducks.

much of his journey on the Pacific, and presented me with five new species of birds obtained by himself, and which are named after him."

Audubon would later name two of the species, the yellow-billed Magpie and the common poorwill, in honor of his friend: *Pica nuttallii* and *Phalaenoptilus nuttallii.*

On October 23, he wrote Bachman, telling him to open his eyes and put on his spectacles: "I have bought Ninety-Three Bird Skins! Yes 93 Bird Skins!—What are they? Why nought less than 93 bird skins from the Rocky Mountains and Columbia River by Nuttall and Townsend!—Cheap as dirt too—Only one hundred and eighty four dollars for the whole of these, and hang me if you don't echo my saying so when *you see them!!* Such beauties! Such rarities! Such novelties!"

When the Charleston cholera quarantine ended in late October, John James and Johnny headed south. They stopped in Washington, DC, along the way to meet with President Andrew Jackson, who invited them to dinner with his family. The next day the Treasury secretary authorized Audubon to travel on revenue cutters anywhere between Chesapeake Bay and the Sabine River at the Texas-Louisiana border. The Treasury secretary also gave Audubon the use of the *Campbell*, a new, speedy sailing cutter moving from Mobile, Alabama, west along the Gulf Coast. Its commander, Napoleon Coste, had been the first officer of the *Marion* on Audubon's journey in Florida and knew both Audubon and his needs.

By now it was possible to travel from Washington to Charleston via train. They arrived on Nov-

Audubon got word that skins of birds collected by Townsend and Nuttall had been sent to the Philadelphia Academy of Science. He knew that these would not be available for him to examine because of George Ord's animosity toward him. But he was heartened to hear that Townsend had duplicates that he might be able to buy. His friend Edward Harris offered $500 to go toward their purchase.

Audubon headed north to Boston, where he met with friends such as Edward Everett, now Governor of Massachusetts, a young ornithologist named Thomas Brewer, and most importantly, Thomas Nuttall, just back from his journey west.

After his meeting with Nuttall, he wrote to Lucy, "September 22, This has been a day of days with me; Nuttall breakfasted with us, and related

ember 17. Johnny and Maria were together again at last!

Birds of the West

Audubon and his younger son spent the winter painting and hunting. Johnny beamed in the presence of his future wife, and Audubon gave life to the new western bird skins in his drawings, completing pictures of 31 species in only 20 days. This was what he had been waiting for. His fourth and final volume of *Birds of America* would feature species from America's west, mostly unknown to ornithologists.

One of those illustrated was a magnificent condor, at that time called a California vulture, an enormous bird with a wingspan of a more than 9 feet (2.7 m). It had been collected by Townsend along the Columbia River, where it was feeding on dead salmon.

Today the bird is called a California condor and is mostly seen in central California. By the 1980s, the populations of this condor had plummeted to only 22 individuals due to illegal hunting, poisoning from lead ammunition, and habitat destruction. A controversial recovery program was initiated that captured wild condors and hosted them in zoos. The young birds were then released into the wild in places like the Sespe Wilderness near Santa Barbara, California. By 2019 the population has risen to a total of more than 500, with 337 in the wild.

As Audubon feverishly worked on illustrating these new western bird species, he waited for word that he could join Captain Napoleon Coste on the revenue cutter *Campbell* for a journey along the Gulf Coast. The trip had been delayed by the ongoing war between the Seminole Indians and the US Army in Florida.

By the end of March 1837, Edward Harris, John James Audubon, and John Woodhouse Audubon

California condor.

Jay Identification

The bird family Corvidae *includes ravens, crows, magpies, jays, and the Clark's nutcracker, some of which are shown in Audubon's illustration. There are 10 species of jays in North America, multiple species of crows and ravens, and two species of magpie. Corvids are highly intelligent, vocal, and most are not shy around people.*

YOU WILL NEED:

↘ Audubon's illustration featuring jays, a magpie, and a Clark's nutcracker

↘ Bird-Watching Journal

↘ Pen or pencil

Which corvids have you seen in your community? Make a list of those you have seen and describe their behavior in your Bird-Watching Journal.

Compare the corvids you observed to those in Audubon's illustration. Do you think you saw one of the species he featured?

From top to bottom: California jay, Steller's jay, yellow-billed magpie, two Clark's nutcrackers.

had rendezvoused with the *Campbell* along the Gulf Coast. Stopping at sandy islands along the coast of Louisiana, the three men hired hunters. Sometimes Captain Coste shot some of the numerous birds migrating north to their summer breeding grounds. Harris noted that during only three days they had shot 104 separate species, but frustratingly for Audubon, none were the species he sought to illustrate for *Birds of America*.

While anchored two miles (3.2 km) below New Orleans on the Mississippi River, Audubon recorded the presence of sandhill cranes, green- and blue-winged teal, and ring-billed gulls. They then sailed to Galveston, where they searched Galveston Bay for new species without success, and Audubon became fatigued slogging through muddy, mosquito-filled marshes. No longer immune to such harsh exercise, his legs swelled "until they were purple."

In a letter to Thomas Brewer, Audubon wrote, "We have found not one new species, but the mass of observations that we have gathered . . . had, I think. Never been surpassed." Every day brought new experiences and knowledge to this student of nature. These observations proved invaluable to his next two volumes of *Ornithological Biography*.

During their overland journey back from New Orleans, both father and son could think of not much more than their return to Charleston. By the time they arrived at the Bachman home, Audubon was 15 pounds lighter than when he left and weary of travel.

Having waited for two years, 21-year-old Johnny and 19-year-old Maria were joined in marriage in May. Now Bachman and Audubon were family as well as dear friends.

In late June, Maria, Johnny, and John James left Charleston. John James went on to visit Edward Harris in Moorestown, New Jersey, while Johnny and Maria continued on to Niagara Falls for their honeymoon.

"Never in my whole life have I enjoyed travelling so much as I have with my beloved daughter," Audubon wrote in a letter to Bachman.

Sandhill crane.

9

THE END IN SIGHT

....

On July 17, 1837 the Audubon family left for Liverpool aboard the packet ship *England*. Enough ice had been loaded that ice cream would be served during the 18-day voyage. How different this was than Audubon's first passage to England from New Orleans, which took 64 days.

The Audubon family was reunited, with the addition of daughter-in-law Maria, at the house on Wimpole Street. Lucy was still not feeling well. Vivacious Maria brought a joy to the family, and she in

Trumpeter swan.

American
flamingos.

turn felt that she fit in well with the Audubons. Johnny, now 25 years old, was able to make a living at portrait painting and took a studio not far away.

Victor was ready to hand over the responsibility of the business to his father. At age 28, he had been indispensable to his father in managing the production and financing of *Birds of America*. No sooner was the family together than Victor took off for the seashore.

Audubon was a loving father who gave his sons responsibility, but not the freedom to set out on their own. He was so consumed by his passion to finish *Birds of America* that he assumed his whole family would unquestionably join him in the work that needed doing. And now that work was approaching the finish line.

Havell thought he might print the final plates by the new year. In October, plate 400 was engraved. It included drawings of five species, the Arkansaw siskin (lesser goldfinch), mealy red-poll (hoary redpoll) a female Louisiana tanager (western tanager), Townsend's bunting (probably a color variant of a dickcissel), and a buff-breasted finch (Smith's longspur).

This group of five is crowded and lacks the elegant composition or background of most of Audubon's illustrations. In a letter to Edward Harris, Audubon wrote, "I am forced to finish my work in as few Numbers of plates as possible (not to lose subscribers in this country). [And therefore] I am forced to introduce as many new species of the same genera in the same plate as circumstances will afford."

On Audubon's explorations of Florida six years earlier, he had watched flamingos from afar but wasn't ever close enough to shoot them. Ever since then, he sought a specimen either preserved in alcohol or a dried skin. Finally he was sent specimens from Cuba preserved in both spirits and dried skins.

American flamingos are almost five feet (1.5 m) tall. The *Birds of America* drawings were printed on the largest sheets of paper at that time called double elephant sheets. Though the pages were big, the flamingo was larger still. Audubon had a challenge to fit a bird almost five feet (1.5 m) tall on a sheet of paper just three and a third feet (1 m) high. In his flamingo print, the bird is bent over in a position similar to one it would take when it was feeding. This visually striking drawing is one of his most popular images.

With the additions of new birds from the northwest collected by Nuttall and Townsend, Audubon needed to have space in his book. The timing was also a challenge because he needed specimens of the new species to draw before they could be included in the book. Originally, he had planned a total of 400 plates. To include new species from the West he would need another 35 plates. These previously unknown species had to be included in the book to make it up-to-date.

Birds of America

By mid-April, Maria was pregnant. The two prospective grandfathers, Bachman and Audubon, were thrilled. And now, Audubon was awaiting not only a grandchild, but also a child of another sort. Begun in 1826, his life's work, *Birds of America*, was about to be fully birthed.

Audubon, seeing the end in sight, finished the artwork for the final 35 plates. One of these, which would be number 406, pictures a trumpeter swan, neck turned backward as if it's about to snatch a butterfly from the water. Being the largest waterfowl in America with a wingspan of 8 feet (2.4 m) and a length of 6 feet (1.8 m), it fills the whole page.

Back in 1810, when he and his business partner Rozier were stalled at an encampment on a river journey to St. Genevieve, they watched and listened to trumpeter swans across the water. This swan's long neck allows it to have a very long windpipe that ends in a saxophone-type loop where it enters the breastbone. Thus, the swan is able to make deep trumpeting calls.

He later wrote that at dusk "the loud-sounding notes of hundreds of Trumpeters would burst on the ear;" and then, "After pluming themselves awhile they would quietly drop their bodies on the ice, and through the dim light I yet could observe the graceful curve of their necks, as they gently turned them backwards, to allow their heads to repose upon the softest and warmest of pillows."

The four massive volumes of *Birds of America* were each 3 feet (0.9 m) tall and 2 feet (0.6 m) wide and weighed around 50 pounds. It took two people to carefully turn the large, thick pages. Within the 435 pages, 497 species were represented in a variety of forms: adults, juveniles, males, females, perched, and in flight. The total number of birds was more than 1,000. The majority of them had been drawn from life by Audubon, and 10 by son John. Backgrounds by Joseph Mason, George Lehman, and Maria Martin placed the birds in landscapes with plants and insects mostly native to each locale.

Page by page, the viewer was guided through a gallery where each picture led to the next, giving an animation-like quality to the experience. The whole was definitely greater than the sum of its parts.

The estimated cost of producing *Birds of America* was $115,640 (equivalent to $3,423,700 in 2020 dollars). Almost all of these funds Audubon earned by his own labors, selling portraits and wildlife scenes, selling bird skins, and selling subscriptions for the book. Robert Havell, his printer, needed payment for his work as well as the work of the colorists who adorned the printed pages. Audubon, explorer and artist, was also a full-time paymaster for a printing company.

Audubon is often portrayed as a failed businessman because of his store in Henderson going bankrupt, but his business was like many other enterprises that couldn't survive the Panic of 1819. However, Audubon accomplished the remarkable feat of making *Birds of America* due to his passion for birds, his amazing physical endurance, and his wife Lucy, who supported herself and the boys on her own for many years. It was as if he created Apple Computers, mostly on his own.

Unfortunately, Audubon was absent from his family for long periods of time and worked long hours painting, overseeing the printing, and corresponding with subscribers. He suffered great losses, such as the destruction by rats of 200 drawings that were in storage. He also lost subscribers during periods of economic instability. In the end, the most serious loss was his remarkable physical strength and endurance.

Between 1826 and 1838, Audubon cultivated support from leading citizens and wealthy individuals in England, France, and the United States, including presidents, members of Congress, and royalty, as well as from influential and knowledgeable scientists. Audubon, despite his occasional arrogance, could charm new acquaintances so that they offered their help and hospitality. His special friends and collaborators—John Bachman, Edward Harris, Richard Harlan, and William MacGillivray—went out of their way to ensure he succeeded in his project. As an explorer describing and naming new species, he also made use of the practice of naming species after supporters. Hence the Harlan's hawk, Harris's sparrow, Bachman's sparrow, and MacGillivray's warbler.

The heavy load that Audubon carried for so many years was almost shed. He still had two more volumes of *Ornithological Biography* to complete and hoped to produce a smaller and more affordable version of *Birds of America*. Off he went to Edinburgh to finish writing *Ornithological Biography*, which was essentially the text for *Birds of America*.

During the summer, he crafted entries on individual birds for Volume 4 of *Ornithological Biography*. Finally, in May 1839 the final volume, Volume 5, was published just five days after Audubon's 54th birthday. Within the five volumes were almost 3,000 pages. Even so, he was not quite finished. He needed to finish the synopsis, a list of all 497 species in scientific order, and a description of five new species that he had found since he had finished Volume 5 of *Ornithological Biography*. This amounted to another 300 pages.

Audubon once wrote in his journals, "I know I am a poor writer. I can scarcely manage to scribble a tolerable English letter, and not much a better one in French. I know I am not a scholar. But I am also aware that no other man living knows better than I do the habits of our birds. No man living has studied them as I have done. I can at least set down plain truths about them, which may be useful and even interesting."

The reviews for *Birds of America* were positive. The *Boston Atlas Newspaper* called it a masterpiece and Audubon a hero for the ages.

Joys and Sorrows

John James and Lucy were ready to go back to America and sailed in August for New York. Victor had left in January for home and was able to rent a house for the family in what today is known as the Tribeca neighborhood of lower Manhattan. In the 1840s, it was considered a fashionable place to live.

Despite final publication of *Birds of America*, the Audubons were still not well off. Audubon had hoped that he would end up with more than 300 subscribers, which would have given them a comfortable income. Over the 14 years since he had first started collecting subscribers, many had dropped out, especially after the depression of 1837. In the end, he had only about 165.

Meanwhile, Victor was in Charleston with the Bachman family. He and Eliza, 9 years his junior, fell in love and were married in autumn 1840. That same season, on September 23, Maria Bachman Audubon died from tuberculosis, leaving her two young daughters, 2-year-old Lulu and 22-month-old Harriet. Audubon, who adored his daughter-in-law, was so brokenhearted he looked to whiskey for solace. He had never had a problem with alcohol. John Bachman, also devastated by his daughter's death, was disgusted by his friend's behavior. Losing a family member from tuberculosis in the 1840s was common. Despite the fact that nearly one in a hundred people died from it, Audubon found it hard to believe his beloved daughter-in-law was gone.

John Woodhouse and John James soon found distraction from their sorrows in new work, *Birds of America: The Royal Octavo Edition*, and John Bachman with the the *Viviparous Quadrupeds of North America*. After finding a suitable printer in Philadelphia, John Woodhouse traveled there to work on reducing his father's life-size drawings to fit in the new smaller *Birds of America* edition. From that point, it could be copied onto stone to make a lithographic print. In this new book, Audubon would correct some errors from *Birds of America*, have only one bird species per plate, and include new species described since the publication of *Birds of America*.

The idea of a smaller version of *Birds of America* was popular, and by April 4, Audubon had 650 subscribers. Finally, Audubon's quarter century of hard work paid off for a profit.

Minnie's Land.
Wellcome Images, WikiCommons

Minnie's Land

If not for the prospects of a new home for the family, the Audubons might have been paralyzed with sadness. Growing on the hilly 24 acres they purchased in northern Manhattan were tall pines, oaks, tulips, and chestnut trees full of singing wood thrushes, chickadees, and robins. The 20 years without a house of her own had been hardest for Lucy. Audubon was happy that he could finally give her that home. He often called her Minnie, an affectionate Scottish word for mother. They called this new home Minnie's Land.

Within a year, the square, two-story, white clapboard house facing the river, with front and back porches and green shutters, was ready for them to move in. The master bedroom was on the second floor, which John James and Lucy would share with their two little granddaughters. Lucy had taken on the role of mother for young Lulu and Harriet. Their father, John Woodhouse, reeling from Maria's death the previous autumn, took long walks alone with the dog.

Lucy knew her son Johnny was feeling better when he introduced them to a young lady he had met and had fallen in love with. Lucy approved of Caroline Hall, the daughter of a Brooklyn merchant. After their marriage on October 2, 1841, the new roomy house would be a blessing for the growing family.

Victor, still wretchedly sad, became interested in Georgianna Mallory, Caroline's close friend.

Soon there would be an orchard full of peach, plum, apricot, pear, and apple trees. As in Hender-

At this time, Victor's wife Eliza was very ill with tuberculosis. By the time Victor and Eliza arrived in New York in mid-May, she was in worse condition and died on May 25. She was only 22 years old. On that day, Audubon had drawn a young gray rabbit nestled near its mother. He later wrote, "I drew this Hare during one of the days of deepest sorrow I have felt in my life." Within a period of eight months both of his sons had lost their wives, who were also their best of friends.

son, they planned to have pigs, poultry, milk cows, and a large garden. The Audubon men all knew this would be Lucy's place.

Like other homes in Audubon's life, it was near a large river trafficked by both cargo and passenger vessels and bordered open space inhabited by birds and other creatures. Across the river were the Palisades, cliffs up to 300 feet (91 m) high along the Hudson's western shore, where peregrine falcons nested on ledges and hunted for ducks along the river. Today the home is part of New York City, located between 155th and 158th Streets, in the southern part of Washington Heights, a heavily Latino community. (In 1842, New York City only extended north to 40th Street.)

On March 2, 1843, Victor Audubon married Georgianna Mallory, a joyous event for the family that had so recently lost two young wives.

Audubon was far from his dream of being free from a nonstop work schedule. He still dreamed of traveling farther west to discover new species of birds and mammals. After trying in vain to get government support for his expedition, he decided to go no matter what. On April 25, 1843, two days before Audubon's 58th birthday, he set off with friend Edward Harris, a master taxidermist, a botanical artist, and an expedition secretary on their journey to the headwaters of the Missouri River. Along the way, Edward Harris shot a "new finch," which later Audubon determined was not yet scientifically named. He named it Harris's finch (now Harris's sparrow). Many weeks later they collected another new finch and named it after his young protégé, Spencer Fullerton Baird.

After reaching their final destination of Fort Union, located near the confluence of the Yellowstone with the Missouri River, they hunted for specimens and explored the surrounding country. One day Audubon and a companion collected the skull of an Indian chief from his burial site, a highly disrespectful and racist action, for Audubon's scientist friend Samuel George Morton, who would measure the brain cavity. Morton believed that "White" races were superior to other races because they had larger brains.

During the expedition, Audubon and Harris failed to collect any new species of mammals. Audubon's heart was not into it, and he was tired. Years of hard work, especially around chemicals had affected his body. He had used arsenic, a poison, to preserve bird skins. His oil paints contained heavy metals like mercury, sulfites, cadmium, and barium, and he was unaware of the danger of these toxic substances. Audubon returned home on November 6, 1843, eight months after leaving, with a meager collection of mammal skins. Wearing a full-grown beard and long hair, he greeted his family with kisses. His new daughter-in-law Georgianna wrote, "he made a fine and striking appearance."

Final Years

Audubon now had a separate studio up the hill from his house and a familiar routine. As in the past, he awoke early to stroll in the woods and watch his "feathered favorites" before breakfasting with the family and then setting to work on illustrations of new bird species for the Octavo edition and mammals for *Viviparous Quadrupeds of North America*. The sales for *Viviparous Quadrupeds of North America* were few, while those for the Octavo edition had topped 1,000.

Audubon was most happy back home surrounded by family. He romped outdoors with little Lulu and Harriet and sang them French songs. He fished, swam in the river, and enjoyed gazing at both the passing barges and ships and the birds flying over and swimming in the river.

Later that year, the Octavo edition was completed. By the time it was finally published, there were 1,100 subscribers, earning Audubon a profit of $36,000 ($1,281,000 in 2021). For once, after many lean years, there was financial security. Despite this, Audubon still felt he needed to earn income from *Viviparous Quadrupeds of North America*.

The following year John's wife, Caroline, gave birth to a baby boy, whom they named John James. He was Audubon's first male grandchild. By year's end, he and Lucy would have a total of five grandchildren, but this joy was tempered by distress. By 1846, Audubon's eyes were failing. He had completed half of the large illustrations for *Viviparous Quadrupeds of North America*, but he could do no more. Audubon had also entered a state of dementia.

This loss of mental abilities such as memory, language, and problem solving would be the end of his work. He had probably suffered some small strokes, and the effects of the toxins from paint and arsenic used in taxidermy had finally taken their toll. He wandered about aimlessly and soon silently withdrew into his own world. Lucy noted, "His eye lost its brightness."

John Woodhouse was away in England with Caroline and the children. When he returned home in May 1847, his father's illness came as a massive shock. Both he and Victor tried their best to hide their father's condition from the public. When Bachman visited the following spring, he understood why he hadn't been receiving letters from his dear friend and wrote to Maria Martin that Audubon's "noble mind is all in ruins." Now John James was merely a quiet presence in the house, sitting silently in the parlor.

Lucy finally had a home of her own at Minnie's Land, surrounded by her sons and their wives and children. After being apart from her husband for most of their married life, she was now with him under the same roof. Tragically, it was as if John James was somewhere else. His body was present, but he was in his own silent world unable to recognize his loved ones. It was clear to everyone that his life was coming to an end.

Lucy's youngest brother, William Bakewell, came to visit from Louisville. As a boy he had often hunted with John James at Henderson. After he greeted John James in his easygoing Kentucky manner, John James's face lit up with recognition, and he spoke, "Yes, yes, Billy! You go down that side of Long Pond, and I'll go down this side, and we'll get the ducks." Audubon was confused, thinking William was a boy, and they were back in Henderson.

These were his last words uttered. Several months later, on January 27, 1851, after days without eating anything, Audubon opened his eyes. He took one long look at Lucy and his sons before he closed his eyes forever. His legendary life of adventure had come to a close. Audubon left behind *Birds of America*, a book like none other past or present, and a family who loved him.

Lucy lived another 23 years, raising her granddaughters and teaching. She outlived both her sons. She died in 1874.

Audubon Lives On

In 1886, one of Lucy's former students, George Bird Grinnell, founded the Audubon Society of New York to protect birds from overhunting. This first state Audubon society did not last long due to lack of funding. Naming it after Audubon, whom he never met but greatly admired, was an honor to his revered former teacher Lucy Audubon. In naming it after Audubon, he kept the memory of him alive for the next century and beyond. This organization would protect birds from the devastation Audubon had witnessed, from excessive hunting, egg gathering, and the transformation of habitat such as canebrakes into farmland.

By the last quarter of the 19th century, there was another severe threat to birds: women's fashion. Using the feathers of wild birds for ornamenting women's hats had become so fashionable that hunters were decimating wild bird populations to meet the demand. The populations of heron, egret, and dozens of other birds were plummeting, and some species like the Carolina parakeet were driven to extinction. Heron

Hats decorated with feathers.
WikiCommons

plumes were sold in packs, averaging 30 ounces, and it took four birds to produce only one ounce of plumes. This led to the slaughter of tens of millions of birds just to meet the needs of hat makers.

In 1896, two Boston socialites, Harriet Hemenway and Minna B. Hall, came to the rescue. Horrified by this carnage, they organized a series of afternoon teas to persuade their high society women friends to stop wearing hats adorned with bird feathers. These meetings led to the creation

Tricolored heron.

By 1905 this informal partnership of state Audubon societies formally became known as the National Association of Audubon Societies. Today it is known as the Audubon Society, and by 2022, it had 600,000 members.

Birds have been the Audubon Society's focus from the start. As one of the largest conservation organizations in the world, it has had a pivotal role in protecting birds and educating the public and government about threats to our bird populations. In 1918 it helped to pass the Migratory Bird Treaty Act, a major step in protecting songbirds as well as waterbirds. This international law was approved by the governments of Canada and Mexico to protect birds that are international residents. As recently as 2017, the Trump administration attempted to weaken the law and the Audubon Society was there to oppose him.

Birds are sensitive to changes in the environment. Poisons used to kill agricultural pests, toxic waste, and human-caused climate change negatively affect birds. Brown pelicans, a species protected in the first National Wildlife Refuge, almost went extinct in the mid-20th century due to DDT, a powerful pesticide used to control mosquitoes and other "pests." Today, brown pelicans are threatened by oil spills, such as the Deepwater Horizon disaster in 2010 that destroyed brown pelican nesting sites and feeding grounds. The Audubon Society and other organizations have come out in opposition to offshore oil drilling.

The society sees climate change as a major threat to not only birds, but also all life on Earth, stating: "Audubon's own science shows that cli-

of the Massachusetts Audubon Society. Within two years, state-level Audubon societies had been established in 15 more states and the District of Columbia. Together these state Audubon societies fought for an end to plume hunting.

By 1901 the Florida Audubon Society had convinced the Florida legislature to pass a law banning the hunting of birds for plumes. That same year, the state Audubon societies helped convince the federal government to establish the Pelican Islands Refuge in Florida, the very first National Wildlife Refuge.

mate change is by far the biggest threat to the birds that we love. That's why Audubon works for solutions to counteract the effects of climate change."

To educate the public about birds, the society offers bird walks and other outdoor programs. It has 41 nature centers, numerous preserves, and a designation for bird habitats that desperately need protection: IBAs (Important Birds Areas). By 2021 it had helped establish almost 3,000 Important Birds Areas in places from the Alaskan Arctic to the Mississippi River Delta, and from Long Island Sound to the Everglades. These cover 417 million acres of public and private lands in the United States. As John James Audubon pointed out, habitats such as canebrakes, old-growth forests, and intact prairie are home to unique species, some of which are now extinct or on the brink of disappearing due to loss of these habitats.

Brown pelican.

Join a Bird Walk

Go birding with people who know the local birdlife. Find out if there is a local Audubon chapter near your community and whether it is hosting any upcoming bird walks. Bird walks are excursions with a knowledgeable leader to locate and observe birds in their natural habitat.

With an adult's permission, visit: www.audubon.org/about/audubon-near-you. Select the state you live in and find a list of local chapters. Hopefully there will be one in your area. If there is no local chapter, see if there is a nature center or local state, county, regional, or national park that offers bird walks. A local land conservancy or other organization may also be worth checking out.

Bring an interested adult, parent, grandparent, or neighbor with you and join a bird walk. Don't forget to bring your Bird-Watching Journal to record your experience.

AFTERWORD

· · · · · · · · · · ·

ORGANIZATIONS LIKE THE Audubon Society, Sierra Club, and others founded more than a century ago by educated "White" men and women have been reexamining their histories and missions. By 2018, they began to listen to critics claiming that they had failed to reach out to non-White communities and their issues.

J. Drew Lanham, a Black American ornithologist and bird-watcher, grew up loving birds and reading all he could about his hero John James Audubon. At the age of eight he became fascinated by birds. "I understood the almost mythical power of Audubon," he wrote. For Lanham, Audubon was the perfect role model—woodsy and heroic, the type of bird-watcher he wished to be. Among other kids playing cowboys or astronauts, he pictured himself dressed in buckskins like Audubon, watching, collecting, and painting birds. But he was Black, and in Kentucky or Louisiana during Audubon's time he would have been a slave, possibly carrying Audubon's gear and supplies.

Lanham remained passionate about birds and became an ornithologist, working as a professor at Clemson University in South Carolina. With the emergence of the civil rights movement, and later "Black Lives Matter" in response to police brutality, Lanham felt a shift. He started reevaluating Audubon the man, and Audubon the organization, in relation to his being Black. Lanham had come across Audubon Society reports from the early 1900s that accused Black people of being for the decline in songbirds and waterfowl. He thought of regional common names still in use, such as "nigger-geese" for the double-crested cormorant. He wondered where he fit in.

Ignoring Audubon's inhumanity as a slaveholder with racist views was no longer acceptable. He faulted Audubon for not trying to be a better person by opposing slavery.

People need heroes and often ignore unheroic qualities of those they choose to admire. Having a passion for birds is human, no matter your race or culture. Organizations like the Audubon Society are now trying to address their past and find ways to support all people with an interest in learning about and defending birds. In 2020, Georgia Audubon hired Corina Newsome, a Black ornithologist, as its community engagement manager to help include underserved non-White community members in Georgia Audubon's programs. In other state Audubon organizations similar programs are being enacted to diversify their membership as they protect the diversity of birds in nature.

RESOURCES

· · · · · · · · · · ·

Sites to Visit

John James Audubon Center at Mill Grove
1201 Pawlings Road
Audubon, Pennsylvania 19403
https://johnjames.audubon.org/
This center at Audubon's first home in America includes a museum about his life and work, and hiking trails. Visitors can participate in bird walks and other special programs.

John James Audubon State Park
3100 US Highway 41
Henderson, Kentucky 42420
https://parks.ky.gov/henderson/parks/historic/john-james-audubon -state-park
This 700-acre wildlife preserve has six miles (9.6 km) of nature trails and a museum hosting one of the largest collections of original Audubon art, plus personal artifacts and memorabilia from Audubon's life.

Audubon State Historic Park
11788 Highway 965
St. Francisville, Louisiana 70775
www.lastateparks.com/historic-sites/audubon-state-historic-site
Visit the site of Audubon's Southern explorations, where he taught and created bird paintings with Mason at the Oakley Plantation in 1821.

Audubon Bird Sanctuary
109 Bienville Boulevard
Dauphin Island, Alabama 36528
This important bird and biodiversity area has three miles (4.8 km) of trails covering 164 acres on the eastern side of Dauphin Island, accessing dunes, pine forest, swamp, and a freshwater lake.

New York Historical Society
170 Central Park West
New York, New York 10024
www.nyhistory.org/exhibitions/audubons-birds-america-focus-gallery
The New York Historical Society has a large collection of Audubon's art, including original *Birds of America* plates and watercolors.

Audubon Mural Project
New York, New York
https://www.audubon.org/amp
Started in 2014, this project has sponsored murals of birds threatened by the climate crisis. As of August 2021, artists have created 90 public murals depicting 127 different bird species around the upper Manhattan neighborhood of Audubon's final home.

Organizations Supporting Birdlife

National Audubon Society

www.audubon.org
Audubon for Kids: *www.audubon.org/get-outside/activities*
/audubon-for-kids
Audubon Camps: *www.audubon.org/httpswwwaudubonorgmenu*
conservation/audubon-camps
The nation's largest bird-centered organization has 23 state programs, 450+ local chapters, and innumerable events. Members can attend birding field trips and presentations, and visit Audubon preserves. Many chapters have youth programs.

American Birding Association

www.aba.org
www.aba.org/connect-with-other-young-birders/
The American Birding Association inspires all people to enjoy and protect wild birds. It offers a simple birding code of ethics and maintains the official checklist for birds of the continental United States, Canada, the French islands of St. Pierre and Miquelon, and adjacent waters to a distance of 200 miles (322 km) from land. The association offers a mentoring program, a young birder of the year program, a list of young birder clubs and young birder camps, and a free electronic birding book.

American Bird Conservancy

https://abcbirds.org/glass-collisions/resources/
Learn how to protect birds from window collision injuries.

Partners in Flight

https://partnersinflight.org/
PIF (Partners in Flight) is a partnership of more than 150 organization in the Americas. They work to protect birds in Canada, the United States, and Mexico. Their website includes tips for birders on personal bird conservation actions.

Royal Society for the Protection of Birds

www.rspb.org.uk
This is the largest organization committed to protecting birds in the United Kingdom through preserving crucial bird habitat, citizen campaigns, education, and scientific monitoring.

Aves Argentinas

www.avesargentinas.org.ar
This Argentine non-profit organization is dedicated to conservation and birding.

NOTES

···········

Introduction

"river pirate" and *"long, murderous-looking knife"*: Richard Rhodes, *John James Audubon: The Making of an American* (New York: Alfred A. Knopf, 2005), 114.

"man of scrupulous honesty": Rhodes, 115.

"I suddenly found myself sunk in quicksand": John James Audubon, *Ornithological Biography, Volume 1* (Philadelphia: Judah Dobson, 1831), 115.

1. A Revolutionary Childhood

"I felt an intimacy" and *"He would point out"*: Audubon, *Ornithological Biography, Volume 1*, vi.

2. New World, New Life

"Hunting, fishing, drawing" and *"And there I sat"*: Maria R. Audubon, *Audubon and His Journals, Volume 1* (New York: Scribner, 1897), 18.

"The genial rays of the sun shine": Audubon, "Plate 7: Purple Grakle, or Common Crow Blackbird," *Birds of America*, accessed January 27, 2022, https://www.audubon.org/birds-of-america/purple-grakle-or-common-crow-blackbird.

"I fixed, a light silver thread": Maria R. Audubon and Elliott Coues, *Audubon and His Journals, Volume 1 and 2* (New York: Scribner's Sons, 1897), 108.

"rash and inconsiderate": Maria R. Audubon, *Audubon and His Journals, Volume 1*, 22.

"Nothing, after all, could ever answer": Rhodes, *Making of an American*, 12.

"Down it I went" and *"My senses must"*: Maria R. Audubon, *Audubon and His Journals, Volume 1*, 21.

"I am here in the Snears": Rhodes, *Making of an American*, 26.

3. Abundance

"My young wife, who possessed talents": Carolyn E. DeLatte, *Lucy Audubon: A Biography* (Baton Rouge: Louisiana State University Press, 1982), 50.

"The nest is of a": Audubon, *Ornithological Biography, Vol. 1*, 233.

"the sun was going down behind the Silver Hills": Audubon, 419.

"When taken by the hand": Audubon, 346.

"Fore part of the head and the cheeks": Audubon, "Plate 26: Carolina Parrot," *Birds of America*, accessed January 28, 2022, https://www.audubon.org/birds-of-america/carolina-parrot.

"really dreadful" and *"rocks and stumps or roots of trees"*: DeLatte, *Lucy Audubon: A Biography*, 66.

"as if walking on a smooth sheet": Audubon, *Ornithological Biography, Vol. 1*, 240.

"The burning heat" through *"gaily, as if nothing"*: Audubon, xiv.

"All at once—like a torrent—and with the noise of thunder": Audubon, *Audubon, By Himself*, ed. Alice Ford (Garden City, NY: Natural History Press), 70.

"To repay evil with kindness": Maria R. Audubon, *Audubon and His Journals, Volume 1*, 344.

4. Losses and Successes

"Up went the mill" and *"Of all the follies of man"*: Audubon, *Audubon, By Himself*, 79.

"expressly for the purpose": Audubon, *Ornithological Biography, Vol. 1*, 456.

"One of the most extraordinary things": Maria R. Audubon, *Audubon and His Journals, Volume 1*, p. 39.

"Nothing was left to me but my humble talents": Rhodes, *Making of an American*, 144.

"the expedition of Major Long" through *"and well do I recollect"*: Maria R. Audubon, *Audubon and His Journals, Volume 1*, 37.

"I never saw this species alight on trees": Audubon, *"Plate 70: Henslow's Bunting," Birds of America*, accessed January 14, 2022, https://www.audubon.org/birds-of-america/henslows-bunting.

"Having a tolerably large number of drawings": Rhodes, *Making of an American*, 145.

"The style & execution of these paintings": Jeff Seuss, "Our History: Time Here Pushed Audubon to Make 'Birds of America,'" *Cincinnati Enquirer*, May 31, 2017, https://www.cincinnati.com/story/news/2017/05/31/cincy-museum-experience-encouraged-audubon-make-birds-america/341440001/.

"Being extremely desirous of settling the long-agitated question": Audubon, *Ornithological Biography, Vol. 1*, 355.

"Without any money": Christoph Irmscher, ed., *John James Audubon: Writings and Drawings* (New York: Library of America, 1999), 3.

"I wish, kind reader": Audubon, "Plate 66: Ivory-billed Woodpecker," *Birds of America*, accessed January 14, 2022, https://www.audubon.org/birds-of-america/ivory-billed-woodpecker.

"I have often seen them after hearing": Irmscher, *Writings and Drawings*, 58.

"I am aboard a keelboat": Francis Hobart Herrick, *Audubon the Naturalist: A History of His Life and Time* (New York: D. Appleton and Co., 1917), 96.

"If this is not the winter retreat of all": Irmscher, *Writings and Drawings*, 66.

"The Rich Magnolia covered": Irmscher, 104.

"It keeps in perpetual motion": Audubon, "Plate 40: American Redstart," *Birds of America*, accessed January 14, 2022, https://www.audubon.org/birds-of-america/american-redstart.

"I feared my hopes of becoming known": Lucy Bakewell Audubon, *The Life of John James Audubon, the Naturalist* (New York: Putnam, 1869), 92.

"Often the blue jay, Thrush": Audubon, *Audubon, By Himself*, 199.

5. Taking a Leap

"It was early, but I found": Audubon, *Audubon, By Himself*, 134.

"flapping their wings 6 or 7 times in quick succession": Alice Ford, ed., *The 1826 Journals of John James Audubon* (New York: Abbeville Press, 1967), 35.

"Raising and falling with such beautiful ease": Ford, 36.

"He praised my drawings and I bowed": Ford, 122.

"Every object known to me smiles": Ford, 123.

"My god I never saw" and *"says he will, with my permission"*: Maria R. Audubon, *Audubon and His Journals, Volume 1*, 153.

"All were, he said, wonderful" and *"Mr. Audubon, the people here"*: Maria R. Audubon, 156.

"A magic power transported us": Herrick, *Audubon the Naturalist*, 360.

"I go to dine" and *"My situation in Edinburgh"*: Herrick, 361.

"Millions of songsters will be drove away": Maria R. Audubon, *Audubon and His Journals, Volume 1*, 182.

"They seem indeed as if created for the purpose": Audubon, "Plate 385: Bank Swallow and Violet-green Swallow," *Birds of America*, accessed January 14, 2022, https://www.audubon.org/birds-of-america/bank-swallow-and-violet-green-swallow.

"like the Mouth of an immense monster": Maria R. Audubon, *Audubon and His Journals, Volume 1*, 251.

"That's the one for me" and *"Well then send for"*: Rhodes, *Making of An American*, 293.

"This morning I took one of my drawings": Maria R. Audubon, *Audubon and His Journals, Volume 1*, 283.

"longed to look at a blue sky": Rhodes, *Making of an American*, 307.

"Mr. Audubon, you are the king": Lucy Bakewell Audubon, *The Life of John James Audubon, the Naturalist*, 179.

"the most magnificent monument": Lucy Bakewell Audubon, 136.

6. The Busy Backwoods Artist

"[The blackpoll warbler] enters Louisiana as early as": Audubon, "Plate 133: Black-poll Warbler," *Birds of America*, accessed January 28, 2022, https://www.audubon.org/birds-of-america/black-poll-warbler.

"There I had the good fortune to be received": Maria R. Audubon, *Audubon and His Journals, Volume 2* (New York: Scribner, 1897), 312.

"It sings sweetly, and at times for half an hour": Audubon, "Plate 94: Grass Finch, or Bay-winged Bunting," *Birds of America*, accessed January 27, 2022, https://www.audubon.org/birds-of-america/grass-finch-or-bay-winged-bunting.

"Trees one after another": Audubon, *Ornithological Biography, Vol. 1*, 55.

"tolerably abundant": Audubon, 56.

"I am at work and have done much": Maria R. Audubon, *Audubon and His Journals, Volume 1*, 61.

"I returned yesterday from Mauch Chunk": Maria R. Audubon, 62.

"The slowness of the stages": Herrick, *Audubon the Naturalist*, 427.

"When I see that no longer any": Irmscher, *Writings and Drawings*, 523.

"I held her in my arms": Maria R. Audubon, *Audubon and His Journals, Volume 1*, 63.

7. New Work, New Honors, and Problems

"It is the facts, the observation": Patricia Tyson Stroud, *The Emperor of Nature* (Philadelphia: University of Pennsylvania Press, 2000), 115–116.

"Writing now is the order of the day": Lucy Bakewell Audubon, *The Life of John James Audubon, the Naturalist*, 205.

"While once sitting in the woods" Audubon, *Ornithological Biography, Volume 1*, 9.

"The nest is nearly of the size and shape of a cocoa-nut": Audubon, 500.

"and so the manuscript went on increasing": Lucy Bakewell Audubon, *The Life of John James Audubon, the Naturalist*, 205–206.

"Mr. Audubon, accept this from me": Lucy Bakewell Audubon, 103.

"country bounded as is always": Rhodes, *Making of an American*, 350.

"a crack!": Howard Corning, ed., *Letters of John James Audubon, 1826–1840* (Boston: The Club of Odd Volumes, 1930), 143.

"hawk of great size, entirely new": Corning, 154.

"Plato was now our guide": Audubon, *Ornithological Biography, Vol. 2*, 294.

"Since then I have heard as many as five or six": Audubon, 366.

"To procure their food, the Spoonbills": Audubon, "Plate 321: Roseate Spoonbill," *Birds of America*, accessed January 27, 2022, https://www.audubon.org/birds-of-america/roseate-spoonbill.

"Rose-colored Curlews (curlew sandpipers) stalked": Maria R. Audubon, *Audubon and His Journals, Volume 2*, 364.

"At three o'clock we started. . . . Our boats were hauled": Rhodes, *Making of an American*, 365.

"Mr. Audubon is the most enthusiastic": Rhodes, 365.

"They had already laid in a cargo": Audubon, *Ornithological Biography, Vol. 3*, 268.

"The Land Bird flits from bush to bush": Audubon, xi.

"The hold of the vessel has been floored": Audubon, 584.

"I am Audubon again": Rhodes, *Making of an American*, 381.

"We are well provided as to clothes": Corning, *Letters of John James Audubon, 1826–1840*, 226.

"the worst of all dreadful bays": Maria R. Audubon and Elliott Coues, *Audubon and His Journals, Volume 1 and 2*, 350.

"These birds certainly are the swiftest": Maria R. Audubon and Coues, 357.

"Until that moment this Tern": Audubon, *Ornithological Biography, Vol. 7*, 107.

"I rubbed my eyes, took my spy-glass": Maria R. Audubon and Coues, *Audubon and His Journals, Volume 1 and 2*, 360.

"The stench from the rock": Maria R. Audubon and Coues, 400.

"were in immense numbers, flying in long files": Maria R. Audubon and Coues, 364.

"The Wild Goose is an excellent diver": Maria R. Audubon and Coues, 373.

"We heard to-day that a party of four men": Lucy Bakewell Audubon, *The Life of John James Audubon, the Naturalist*, 315.

"The Turdus migratorius must be the hardiest": Maria R. Audubon and Coues, *Audubon and His Journals, Volume 1 and 2*, 379.

"resembles the clicking of small pebbles": Maria R. Audubon and Coues, 381.

"sweet notes of this bird": Maria R. Audubon and Coues, 382.

"We found more wildness in this species": Audubon, *Ornithological Biography, Vol. 1*, 539–540.

"It was a beautiful morning when I arose": Maria R. Audubon and Coues, *Audubon and His Journals, Volume 1 and 2*, 420.

"Seldom in my life have I left": Maria R. Audubon and Coues, 284.

"We were now, thanks to God": Maria R. Audubon and Coues, 288.

8. Back to Bachman, and Then England

"The young were three" and *"none of the numerous"*: Audubon, *Ornithological Biography, Volume 2*, 402.

"as good as any I ever made": Corning, *Letters of John James Audubon, 1826–1840*, 274.

"nearly 100 drawings of water birds ready for publication": Corning, *Letters of John James Audubon, 1826–1840*, 274.

"The rows of trees about the plantations are full of them": Audubon, *Ornithological Biography, Vol. 2*, 304.

"for my part I would rather go without a shirt": Corning, *Letters of John James Audubon, 1826–1840*, 334.

"He [Audubon] has told what he has seen": Stanley Arthur, *Audubon: An Intimate Life of the American Woodsman* (New Orleans: Harmanson, 1937), 428.

"September 22, This has been a day of days": Lucy Bakewell Audubon, *The Life of John James Audubon, the Naturalist*, 393.

"until they were purple": Lucy Bakewell Audubon, 409.

"We have found not one new species": Arthur, *American Woodsman*, 442.

"Never in my whole life": Corning, *Letters of John James Audubon, 1826–1840*, 1.

9. The End in Sight

"I am forced to finish my work": Rhodes, *Making of an American*, 402.

"After pluming themselves awhile": Audubon, *Ornithological Biography, Volume 1*, 538.

"I know I am a poor writer": Maria R. Audubon, *Audubon and His Journals, Volume 1*, 64.

"I drew this Hare during one of the days": Rhodes, *Making of an American*, 415.

"he made a fine and striking appearance": Rhodes, 430.

"His eye lost its brightness": Rhodes, 432.

"noble mind is all in ruins": Maria R. Audubon, *Audubon and His Journals, Volume 1*, 76.

"Yes, yes, Billy!": Rhodes, *Making of an American*, 434.

Afterword

"I understood the almost mythical power": J. Drew Lanham, "What Do We Do About John James Audubon?" *Audubon Magazine*, spring 2021, https://www.audubon.org/magazine/spring-2021/what-do-we-do-about-john-james-audubon.

SELECTED BIBLIOGRAPHY

· · · · · · · · · · ·

Adams, Alexander B. *John James Audubon: A Biography.* New York: Putnam, 1966.

Arthur, Stanley. *Audubon: An Intimate Life of the American Woodsman.* New Orleans: Harmanson, 1937.

Audubon, John James. *Audubon, By Himself.* Edited by Alice Ford. Garden City, NY: Natural History Press, 1969.

Audubon, John James. *Ornithological Biography.* 5 vols. Philadelphia: Judah Dobson publisher, 1831–1839.

Audubon, Lucy Bakewell, *The Life of John James Audubon, the Naturalist.* New York: Putnam, 1869.

Audubon, Maria R., and Elliott Coues. *Audubon and His Journals, Volume 1 and 2.* New York: Scribner's Sons, 1897.

Corning, Howard. *Letters of John James Audubon, 1826–1840.* Boston: The Club of Odd Volumes, 1930.

DeLatte, Carolyn E. *Lucy Audubon, A Biography.* Baton Rouge: Louisiana State University Press, 1982.

Dock, George, Jr. *Audubon's Birds of America.* New York: Harry N. Abrams, 1979.

Ford, Alice, ed. *The 1826 Journals of John James Audubon.* New York: Abbeville Press, 1967.

Ford, Alice. *John James Audubon, A Biography.* New York: Abbeville Press, 1988.

Foshay. Ella M. *John James Audubon.* New York, Harry N. Abrams, 1997.

Herrick, Francis Hobart. *Audubon the Naturalist: A History of His Life and Time.* 2 vols. New York: Appleton-Century Company, 1917.

Irmscher, Christoph, ed. *John James Audubon, Writings and Drawings.* New York: Library of America, 1999.

Proby, Kathryn Hall. *Audubon in Florida.* Coral Gables, FL: University of Miami Press, 1974.

Rhodes, Richard. *John James Audubon: The Making of an American.* New York: Alfred A. Knopf, 2005.

Souder, William. *Under a Wild Sky: John James Audubon and the Making of the Birds of America.* New York: North Point, 2004.

Streshinsky, Shirley. *Audubon: Life and Art in the American Wilderness.* Athens, GA: University of Georgia Press, 1993.

Stroud, Patricia Tyson. *The Emperor of Nature.* Philadelphia: University of Pennsylvania Press, 2000.

INDEX

· · · · · · · · · · ·